ALCOHOL AND THE ELDERLY

ALCOHOL AND THE ELDERLY
A COMPREHENSIVE BIBLIOGRAPHY

Compiled by Grace M. Barnes,
Ernest L. Abel, and Charles A. S. Ernst

GREENWOOD PRESS

WESTPORT, CONNECTICUT • LONDON, ENGLAND

Library of Congress Cataloging in Publication Data

Barnes, Grace M
    Alcohol and the elderly.

    Includes index.
    1. Aged—Alcohol use—Bibliography. I. Abel,
Ernest L., 1943–   joint author. II. Ernst,
Charles A. S., joint author. III. Title.
Z7721.B36   [HV5138]   362.2'92'0880565   80-1786
ISBN 0-313-22132-4 (lib. bdg.)

Library of Congress Catalog Card Number: 80-1786
ISBN: 0-313-22132-4

First published in 1980

Greenwood Press
A division of Congressional Information Service, Inc.
88 Post Road West, Westport, Connecticut 06881

Printed in the United States of America

10 9 8 7 6 5 4 3 2 1

Contents

Preface

In recent years alcohol-related problems among the elderly have received growing critical attention. During the past ten years, in particular, the number of articles, books, reports, and monographs focusing on the significance of alcohol consumption among the aged has greatly increased. Studies range from definition and classification of elderly drinkers to alcohol-related health problems among the aged; from the need for improvement of health care facilities to the use of alcohol as a form of geriatric therapy; and from surveys of drinking patterns of various populations to comparative experiments with old and young laboratory animals.

The following bibliography brings together over twelve hundred pertinent references cited in *The Journal of Studies on Alcohol, Index Medicus, Current Contents*, and numerous other sources relating to these issues. Although the majority of the citations are dated 1970 or later, this bibliography includes references from the 1920s to the present. While other computerized literature searches on the topic of alcohol and the elderly may list an article if both alcohol and the aged are mentioned in the article, even if these two categories are not directly linked to each other in the given work, the items in the present bibliography include only those references which directly link alcohol consumption to an elderly population, subgroup, or case study. In the human studies cited, the age criterion for inclusion has generally been fifty-five years and above. Studies which do not appear by title to be directly related to alcohol and aging have been included only after careful review of an informative abstract and, in most cases, the article itself. For example, drinking surveys among general populations have been included if patterns of consumption are reported specifically for older age groups. Finally, studies of drugs and the elderly are listed only if alcohol is among the drugs discussed.

Although every attempt has been made to make this bibliography the most comprehensive source of citations to the literature on alcohol and the elderly, it is not exhaustive. For example, items in general newspapers, newsletters, or some popular magazines may have been inadvertently omitted.

Items listed in this bibliography are arranged alphabetically by last name of author. Titles which did not appear in English are listed according to the original language and with an English translation. Journal titles are expanded for clarity. All entries are consecutively numbered and are cataloged by number in the subject index.

The authors give special thanks to Diane Augustino, librarian at the Research Institute on Alcoholism, for her help and cooperation in gathering together pertinent information for this work. The authors also gratefully acknowledge the assistance of Hebe B. Greizerstein in translating many of the titles which are cited in this bibliography.

The significance and scope of the problems associated with alcohol and the elderly make this area a fruitful one for continued attention. To that end, we hope that this bibliography will be a useful aid to future study.

Introduction

Growing public concern has been directed in recent years at the use and abuse of alcohol and other drugs among the elderly. The proportion of adults aged sixty-five years and older has been increasing in recent decades and presently the elderly constitute approximately 10 percent of the U.S. population. Because advanced age often brings declining health, the elderly utilize medical services and medications out of proportion to their numbers. It is estimated that the elderly consume approximately 25 percent of the nation's prescription drugs. Thus, in addition to the important primary effects of alcohol on biological and social functioning, the use of alcohol combined with these other drugs creates an increased potential for serious adverse reactions to which the aged are particularly vulnerable.

BIOLOGICAL ASPECTS OF ALCOHOL CONSUMPTION AMONG THE ELDERLY

Because of biological changes associated with aging, it is likely that use of alcohol or other drugs in amounts that are relatively safe in younger populations may produce adverse and unexpected reactions in the elderly. Among the many physiological changes associated with aging that could influence alcohol and other drug responsiveness are a decrease in drug metabolizing activity as a result of changes in liver function, a decrease in drug elimination rates due to changes in kidney function, an increase in the concentration of drugs in the blood due to reduced fluid volume and mass, and altered responsiveness of target organs such as the brain.

Despite growing awareness that aging affects responsiveness to alcohol and other drugs, very little has been done to identify which substances, in what doses and combinations, in fact pose a danger to the elderly person. The problem has become so acute in recent years that the National Institute on Aging recently identified idiosyncratic drug reactions among the elderly as a major research question. The question of increased responsiveness to drugs is an especially important problem in the case of alcohol, which has traditionally been the most widely used and abused drug among the U.S. population.

Absorption, Distribution, Metabolism, and Elimination of Alcohol

Although alcohol is absorbed from the stomach into the blood stream, the primary site of absorption is the small intestine. While absorption tends to be rapid, the presence of food in the stomach has the effect of slowing the rate of absorption by delaying the movement of alcohol from the stomach into the blood, and from the stomach into the intestine.

Once absorbed in the blood, alcohol is distributed to various organs in accordance with their blood supply. Tissues with a rich blood supply, such as the brain, liver, and kidney, rapidly attain levels of alcohol equal to that in the blood, whereas tissues with poor blood supply, such as skeletal muscle and fat, take much longer to attain equilibrium with the blood.

Most of the alcohol in the body is metabolized in the liver by the enzyme, alcohol dehydrogenase (ADH). This enzyme converts the alcohol to acetaldehyde and ultimately to carbon dioxide and water. Only about 10 percent of the absorbed alcohol is directly eliminated in unmetabolized form through the lungs, kidneys, and sweat glands, whereas vast amounts are oxidized in the liver.

The concentration of alcohol in the blood is typically stated in terms of milligrams or grams of alcohol in 100 milliliters of blood. For example, 25 milligrams of alcohol per 100 milliliters of blood would constitute a blood alcohol level (BAL) of 25 mg. percent or .025 g. percent. (Since gram percent is almost always used in assessing intoxication, BAL is generally stated simply as .025 percent.) Although each state has its own BAL criterion for intoxication, most states have set a BAL of 0.10 percent or 0.15 percent as the minimum level for intoxication. Below a 0.10 percent BAL, coordination, vision, hearing, and speech may be somewhat impaired in the average adult but many states do not regard this impairment to be great enough to be termed "legal intoxication." Above a BAL of 0.15 percent, coordination and sensory acuity are seriously compromised and there is no question of drunkenness. At a BAL of 0.20 percent, motor control is almost completely lost and mental confusion usually occurs.

In animal studies, where the amount of alcohol and other relevant factors associated with alcohol use can be better manipulated and controlled than in human studies, older animals have been found to be affected to a much greater extent than younger animals after receiving equal amounts of alcohol. For example, older animals sleep longer, their motor activity is more impaired, and their body temperatures are lowered to a greater extent than younger animals. Older animals are also far more susceptible to the toxic effects of alcohol.

This greater susceptibility of older animals to the effects of alcohol may be due in part to a greater susceptibility of the central nervous system to alcohol as aging progresses. However, it is also likely that the greater impact of alcohol in older animals is due to the fact that blood alcohol levels become much higher in older animals even when young and old animals of the same weight receive the same amount of alcohol. This is because older animals have far less body water and less lean body mass in relation to total body mass. As a result, the older animal has a smaller volume of distribution for substances that are distributed into body water. Since alcohol is distributed throughout the body in accordance with total body water and distribution is not appreciably affected by body fat, blood alcohol levels are much higher in the older animal. Thus, the greater impact of alcohol associated with aging may be due to differences between old and young animals in body composition. Since the same kind of bodily changes associated with aging occur in the human body as in other animals, elderly humans can also be expected to be affected by equal amounts of alcohol to a greater extent than younger adults. In other words, an older adult may become intoxicated after drinking less alcohol than a younger counterpart.

Although the elderly differ from their younger counterparts in terms of absorption and distribution of alcohol in the body, there does not appear to be any differences in the rate of elimination of alcohol from the body. This suggests that liver and kidney functions with respect to the metabolism and elimination of alcohol are not affected by old age.

Tolerance and Dependence

Aging is associated with a decreased resiliency in nearly all body systems, resulting in a greater sensitivity to most substances, including alcohol. However, exceptions to this generalization are those elderly persons who have a relatively sustained pattern of heavy drinking and who may have developed a considerable degree of tolerance to alcohol.

Chronic use of alcohol can result in a doubling of the metabolic rate. The increased rate of metabolism resulting from chronic use of alcohol, termed metabolic tolerance, is due to the induction and/or accelerated rate of activity of alcohol dehydrogenase, which converts alcohol to acetaldehyde.

In addition to metabolic tolerance, the brain itself may become tolerant to the effects of alcohol following chronic drinking so that more alcohol is required to produce the same effect that was produced previously by less alcohol. This kind of tolerance, called functional tolerance, is believed to be due to an adaptation of nerve cells to the presence and effects of alcohol.

As a further result of both metabolic and functional tolerance, alcoholics may be less affected by other drugs, such as sedative-hypnotic drugs and general anesthetics, taken in the absence of alcohol. This decreased responsiveness, termed cross-tolerance, can also occur in the other direction. Individuals tolerant to sedative-hypnotic drugs such as the barbiturates, for example, may also be tolerant to alcohol. However, while it may require more alcohol to produce intoxication, or more barbiturate to produce sedation, the lethal dose of these substances may not likewise increase. Consequently, the development of tolerance may result in accidental death due to drug overdose. Accidental death may also occur as a result of the interaction of alcohol with other drugs, since the combined effects of these drugs may be greater than the additive effects of these drugs taken individually.

Tolerance to alcohol is generally linked with dependence. The degree of dependence is indicated by the severity of a withdrawal syndrome which occurs following cessation of chronic drinking. Initially, withdrawal causes feelings of anxiety, irritability, insomnia, and uncontrollable shaking. These symptoms last for about twenty-four to forty-eight hours and then subside. During this period, hallucinations may also be experienced. Recovery is often rapid after this initial withdrawal period. However, in cases of chronic and prolonged drinking, withdrawal symptoms may be especially severe, including delirium, disorientation, paranoia, agitation, fever, diarrhea, vomiting, and convulsive seizures. This period of "delirium tremens" peaks at about three days after abstinence and can last for several more days. Withdrawal is sometimes so severe that the patient eventually dies.

It can be speculated that the older the patient, the less likely that she/he will be able to withstand the stress of withdrawal. Furthermore, the withdrawal syndrome may not be readily recognized since many of the signs and symptoms are the same as those associated with senility, dementia, or other conditions related to the aging process.

Nutrition

Alcohol is a source of calories (7cal/gram) and as such may substitute for caloric intake from other food sources, resulting in overall undernutrition. Since aging is associated with reduced appetite and/or food consumption, altered eating habits, and undernutrition resulting from lower income and hence lower expenditures for food, the nutritional effects of alcohol consumption may be compounded in the elderly.

In addition, alcohol affects the absorption and utilization of nutrients in the body. For example, alcohol has been shown to inhibit absorption of thiamine from the intestine (an effect which may be responsible for the thiamine deficiency frequently observed among alcoholics), along with riboflavin, niacin, and folic acid. Fat absorption from the intestine is likewise impaired. Excessive alcohol intake also results in damage to various organs of the body, such as the liver, resulting in depletion of vitamins stored in these organs (e.g., vitamin A depletion from the liver). Several neurological syndromes, such as Wernicke's disease and Korsafoff's syndrome, that are associated with alcoholism and complicated by the aging process, are believed to be due in part to alcohol-induced vitamin deficiencies. In addition to its effects on absorption of nutrients, alcohol also promotes the loss from the body of essential minerals, such as magnesium, calcium, and zinc.

Other Medical Consequences

Excessive alcohol users have been shown to have exceptionally high rates of morbidity and mortality. Alcohol-related disorders have been linked to virtually all body systems, and include diseases of the heart, the skeletal muscles, the blood, the tissues, the neurological system, and the digestive system, as well as various mental disorders. Although definitive research showing the direct physical effects of alcohol specifically in older persons is lacking, nonetheless, certain conditions, such as heart disease and brain dysfunctions, are overrepresented among elderly persons.

Many of these same disorders are worsened, if not caused by, excessive alcohol consumption. For example, sustained heavy drinking may predispose an individual to the onset of coronary heart disease, such as alcoholic cardiomyopathy, which is believed to be directly caused by the toxic effects of alcohol and its metabolic product, acetaldehyde, on the myocardium. Thus, older persons, with decreased cardiac functioning, sustain a substantially greater chance of developing more serious cardiac problems if they continue to consume alcohol. In fact, some studies report that relatively small amounts of alcohol can significantly raise a person's blood pressure. Even a single drink of an alcoholic beverage may result in decreased cardiac efficiency in persons with a history of heart disease.

Various neural disorders also show clear parallels between the characteristics of the disease in alcoholics and in the elderly. Excessive alcohol consumption contributes to serious cognitive and perceptual deficits and these impairments closely resemble the symptoms of organicity often observed in extreme old age. This has lead a number of investigators to conclude that excessive drinking results in "premature aging" and further, that the neurological consequences of both prolonged heavy drinking and mental aging may have common underlying metabolic or nutritional bases. Unfortunately, many of the studies of neural deficits associated with alcoholism have not been well controlled with regard to age. Future research must address itself to a more definitive understanding of the separate as well as the joint effects of alcoholism and the aging process on neural damage. Nonetheless, from existing evidence it can be concluded that elderly persons, who are experiencing a slowing in reaction time and mental processing, are especially vulnerable to the effects of a central nervous system depressant such as alcohol.

SOCIO-EPIDEMIOLOGIC ASPECTS OF ALCOHOL CONSUMPTION AMONG THE ELDERLY

Prevalence of Elderly Alcohol Use and Abuse

The prevalence of alcohol use and abuse among the elderly varies considerably depending upon the population studied, the methods used, and the criteria chosen to designate heavy drinking, problem drinking, and alcoholism. The definition of heavy drinking, for example, generally refers to a pattern of consumption involving the frequency of drinking along with the quantity usually drunk. Because of the biological aspects of alcohol use among the aged described above, the elderly adult may be far more incapacitated than a younger counterpart even with the same consumption level. Thus, even moderate drinking may be a potential hazard to the health and well-being of certain aged persons.

Although heavy drinking cannot necessarily be equated with problem drinking, heavy drinkers have been shown to have a far greater risk of developing alcohol-related problems, such as marital problems or instances of driving while intoxicated, than do moderate or infrequent drinkers.

If one's criteria for alcoholism include the existence of physical dependence on alcohol to the extent that symptoms of withdrawal appear once drinking is stopped, then obviously the rate of alcohol abuse among the elderly will be far less than if one uses a broader definition of alcohol abuse such as the one adopted by the World Health Organization, which holds that drinking is a problem if it involves impairment of health, economic functioning, or social functioning.

Despite these problems of definition, it has been consistently reported in national and regional cross-sectional surveys that the elderly are more likely to be abstainers than are people in younger age groups in the general population. These same studies show that older adults have lower proportions of heavy drinking and alcohol-related problems than do their younger counterparts. These differences may reflect generational changes; that is, perhaps drinking among the elderly has remained fairly stable while younger people are drinking more today than their parents or grandparents did at the same age. While there may be support for this assumption, there is considerable evidence indicating that many persons decrease their drinking as they become older due to poor health, less social contacts, less discretionary income, and simply, less desire to drink. Furthermore, it has been reported that approximately half of the elderly abstainers were former drinkers. Health reasons and loss of interest in alcohol are primary reasons often cited for giving up drinking.

Several investigators have demonstrated that there is a high rate of "maturing out" of alcohol abuse among those who reach old age. Similarly, alcoholism has been viewed as a potentially "self-limiting disease" in that significant numbers of older alcoholics spontaneously pass through the phase where alcohol impairs their health and social well-being. Thus, the fact that some elderly persons drink less than formerly or give up alcohol entirely no doubt accounts in part for the lower rates reported of heavy drinking and alcohol-related problems among persons over sixty years of age in contrast with the under-sixty group in general population studies.

Moreover, morbidity rates are high among long-time heavy users of alcohol. Thus, one can speculate that older alcohol abusers are less likely than non-abusers to be found living in household settings. This may explain the finding that the rate of alcohol abuse among the elderly in various institutional settings, such as general hospitals or psychiatric facilities, is generally much higher than for the same age group in the general population.

In addition, it is well documented that alcoholics who have a long-existing history of heavy drinking have higher mortality rates than persons of the same age without a background of alcohol abuse. In fact, there are indications that the life span of an alcoholic may be shortened on the average by as much as ten to fifteen years. This may account in part for the relatively low rates of heavy drinking among elderly in household surveys, especially among males over sixty years in contrast to males in mid-life.

Types of Elderly Alcohol Abusers

Although consumption of alcohol is generally lower among the elderly, it has been reported that alcohol abuse may actually increase for certain elderly adults as a means of coping with anxiety and depression resulting from retirement and its associated disruption of domestic life-styles, or to combat the isolation, grief, and other painful accompaniments of old age. Some reports indicate that elderly widowers, for example, are a group particularly susceptible to alcoholism; however, other investigators argue that stresses of aging such as retirement and widowhood are not systematically linked to sharp increases in heavy and problem drinking.

An important question awaiting clarification involves determining the proportion of elderly adults who continue their problem drinking of earlier years versus the number who begin drinking heavily as a result of age-related problems. Is the elderly alcohol abuser a person who has had a drinking problem since younger years, or has she/he become a problem drinker due to emotional stresses associated with aging?

In this regard, two types of elderly alcohol abusers have been characterized: early-onset alcoholics and late-onset alcoholics. Early-onset drinkers, referred to as Type 1 alcoholics, have a long history of alcohol abuse and continue this pattern of excessive drinking into their elderly years. Of elderly alcohol abusers, the majority—some estimate the figure at two-thirds—have been characterized as Type 1. Late-onset drinkers, or Type 2 alcoholics, have been characterized as drinking excessively in reaction to the various stresses associated with the aging process. Some clinicians report that the prognosis for treatment is better with Type 2 drinkers than with Type 1 alcohol abusers since the late-onset excessive drinkers appear to be healthier and more socially stable than their early-onset counterparts.

Other Alcohol-Related Social Problems

Various other social problems that may also be complicated by the aging process have been shown to be linked to excessive alcohol consumption. For example, elderly drivers have been found to have higher than average automobile accident rates. Elderly persons are three times more vulnerable to accidents at low blood alcohol concentrations (.01 percent to .04 percent) than at zero blood alcohol levels, so that drinking and driving is a potentially serious combination for the elderly. Also, the elderly are involved in a disproportionate number of pedestrian accidents and often the role of alcohol is suspect.

The elderly also commit a disproportionate number of suicides; indeed, some estimates indicate that they commit a quarter of all suicides. There is some evidence that alcoholics are also a high risk group for suicide. Conditions precipitating suicide attempts are often the same as the factors associated with aging and with excessive drinking. Some of these factors, which have been mentioned earlier, are failing physical health, the loneliness accompanying death of loved ones or retirement, and declining mental faculties. While there is a lack of definitive research directly linking alcohol abuse among the aged to various social problems, there are enough observations to make this a worthwhile subject for future study.

Beneficial Aspects of Alcohol Use

Most of the literature regarding alcohol consumption among the elderly focuses on the adverse consequences of drinking behavior. However, there are a number of reports linking alcohol use with positive behaviors. For example, elderly persons who are active physically and socially and who are in good health are more likely to drink than those in poor health or those who are less active. (Of course, activity is strongly related to good health.) The drinking described in these situations is likely to be light to moderate social drinking taking place in the context of good health, good psychological well-being, and active social participation.

Moderate drinking may also have beneficial psychological effects for elderly persons in nursing home situations. Experimental studies have shown that not only are there no known ill effects on health from the consumption of small amounts of alcohol, but there are rather clear signs of the psychological benefits of alcohol among geriatric patients, namely, better morale, improved sleep, and a greater sense of overall well-being. Several nursing homes reportedly keep "alcohol therapy" as an ongoing activity after completion of such studies. However, the long-term effects of this type of therapy are unknown.

Identification of Elderly Alcohol Abusers for Treatment

The problem of identifying elderly alcohol abusers no doubt serves as the greatest deterrent to treatment. Heavy drinking among the elderly may not be detected because of denial, either by the individual or by her/his family. Elderly heavy drinkers may also be less visible because they have retired and are no longer in the mainstream of society. Unless they call attention to themselves, for example, as public inebriates, they are less likely to be noticed than younger problem drinkers who are more readily identified through work problems or family difficulties. In addition, many of the symptoms often associated with aging, such as senility or frailty, closely resemble those associated with excessive drinking. Thus, for example, alcoholism may be mistaken for senile dementia, or vice versa.

Elderly patients may be admitted to a treatment facility for a particular physical or psychiatric disorder for which alcohol abuse may in fact be the primary etiological factor. Since these patients are not initially assigned to an alcohol unit, they may be unlikely to receive treatment for their drinking problems. Several studies indicate that among elderly psychiatric patients and among elderly patients in general medical hospital wards, the proportion of persons with alcoholism is high —often as high as 50 percent of all elderly patients.

Another barrier to the treatment of alcohol problems among the elderly is that in many institutions, alcoholism treatment facilities have limited resources and are unable to serve all who need their services. Since alcoholism services are typically aimed at younger adults, the elderly alcoholic is often likely to find inadequate services available. Moreover, elderly alcoholics are often considered to have a poor prognosis and are, therefore, less likely than younger alcoholics to be admitted into treatment programs. However, as noted earlier, those elderly persons who would be characterized as late-onset alcoholics or those reacting to the stresses of aging may indeed respond favorably to treatment. In these instances the treatment might well involve attempts to alter one's life-style to combat such factors as isolation and loneliness by providing more social contacts and support through community agencies for the elderly.

Bibliography

A

1. Abel, Ernest L. Effects of Ethanol and Pentobarbital in Mice of
   Different Ages. Physiological Psychology, 6(3): 366-368,
   1978.

2. Abelsohn, D.S. and van der Spuy, H.I.J. The Age Variable in
   Alcoholism. Journal of Studies on Alcohol, 39(5): 800-808,
   1978.

3. Abelson, H.I., Fishburne, P.M. and Cisin, Ira. National Survey
   on Drug Abuse: 1977. A Nationwide Study--Youth, Young
   Adults, Older People. Volume 1. Main Findings. DHEW Publication No. ADM 78-618. Rockville, Maryland: National Institute on Drug Abuse, 1977.

4. Abrahams, R., Baker, F. and Patterson, R.D. Preventing Self-
   Destructive Behavior. Geriatrics, 29(2): 115-121, 1974.

5. Achte, K., Seppala, K., Ginman, L. and Colliander, N. Alcoholic
   Psychosis in Finland. Helsinki: Finnish Foundation for
   Alcohol Studies, 1969.

6. Adams, Junius. Drink to Your Health: Alcohol without Alcoholism.
   New York: Harper and Row, 1976, especially pages 46-47.

7. Agarwal, M.K., Muthuswamy, P.P., Banner, A.S. and Addington, W.W.
   Occurrence with Bacteriologically Positive Pulmonary Tuberculosis. Journal of the American Medical Association, 238
   (21): 2297-2299, 1977.

8. Aisenberg, R. What Happens to Old Psychologists? A Preliminary
   Report. In: New Thoughts on Old Age. Ed. Robert Kastenbaum. New York: Springer Publishing Co., 1964, pages 116-
   138.

9.   Albot, G. and Parturier-Albot, M. De la signification et des
     conséquences biologiques des diverses anomalies histologiques
     et ultrastructurales observées dans les hépatites alcooliques
     subaiguës. [The Significance and Biological Consequences of
     Various Histological and Ultrastructural Anomalies Observed
     in Subacute Alcoholic Hepatitis.] Semaine des Hôpitaux de
     Paris, 45: 1935-1948, 1969.

10. Albrecht, Gary L. The Alcoholism Process: A Social Learning
     Viewpoint. In: Alcoholism: Progress in Research and Treat-
     ment. Ed. Peter G. Bourne and Ruth Fox. New York and Lon-
     don: Academic Press, 1973, Chapter 2, Part 3: The Problem
     Drinking Process, pages 18-24, especially page 23.

11. Alcohol and Gout. (Queries and Minor Notes.) Journal of the
     American Medical Association, 146: 1089, 1951.

12. Alcohol and Other Drug Problems among Senior Citizens. The Bot-
     tom Line, 2(2): 21-24, 1978.

13. Alcoholism: A Growing Medical-Social Problem. Statistical Bul-
     letin of the Metropolitan Life Insurance Company, 48(4):
     7-10, 1967.

14. Alcohol Problems among the Elderly. The Bottom Line, 2(1): 4-9,
     1979.

15. Allgulander, C. and Borg, S. Sedative-Hypnotic and Alcohol Depen-
     dence among Psychiatric In-Patients. British Journal of
     Addiction, 73(2): 123-128, 1978.

16. Allsop, J. and Turner, B. Cerebellar Degeneration Associated
     with Chronic Alcoholism. Journal of the Neurological Sci-
     ences, 3: 238-258, 1966.

17. Alsumait, A.R., Jabbari, M. and Goresky, C.A. Pancreatico-Col-
     onic Fistula: A Complication of Pancreatitis. Canadian
     Medical Association Journal, 119: 715-719, 1978.

18. Altschule, Mark D., Victor, Maurice and Holliday, Phyllis D.
     Carbohydrate Metabolism in Brain Disease. IX. Carbohydrate
     Metabolism in the Chronic Alcoholic Psychoses. American
     Medical Association Archives of Internal Medicine, 99: 40-
     46, 1957.

19. Amir, Menachem. Sociological Study of the House of Correction.
     American Journal of Corrections, 28(2): 20-24, 1966.

20. Amir, S. Brain and Liver Aldehyde Dehydrogenase Activity and
     Voluntary Ethanol Consumption by Rats: Relations to Strain,
     Sex, and Age. Psychopharmacology, 57(1): 97-102, 1978.

21. Andersen, O.J. Registrering av behovsanalyse blant herbergister
     og bostedsløse alkoholister i Oslo. [Registration of the
     Needs among Lodgers and Alcoholics without Place of Resi-
     dence in Oslo.] Tidsskrift om Edruskaps Spørsmal, 30(2):
     30-32, 1978.

22. Angelini Rota, M. Due casi di intossicazione acuta mortale da
     alcool etilico. [Two Cases of Fatal Acute Ethyl Alcohol
     Poisoning.] Zacchia, 24: 369-387, 1961.

23. Anguera, G. and Schwartz, D. Contribution à l'étiologie des
     troubles vasculaires rétiniens. Etude de certains facteurs,
     notamment l'alcool et le tabac. [Contribution to the Etio-
     logy of Retinal Vascular Disorders. A Study of Certain Fac-
     tors, Particularly Alcohol and Tobacco.] Revue de l'Athero-
     sclerose et des Arteriopathies Peripheriques France (Supple-
     ment to Archives des Maladies du Coeur et des Vaisseaux), 1:
     239-255, 1959.

24. Apfeldorf, Max. The Quantitative Objective Assessment of Per-
     sonality Traits of Alcoholics over the Life Span. Addictive
     Diseases, 3(3): 449-456, 1978.

25. Apfeldorf, Max and Hunley, Phyllis J. Application of MMPI Alco-
     holism Scales to Older Alcoholics and Problem Drinkers.
     Journal of Studies on Alcohol, 36(5): 645-653, 1975.

26. Apfeldorf, Max and Hunley, Phyllis J. The Adjective Check List
     Applied to Older Institutionalized Men. Journal of Per-
     sonality Assessment, 35: 457-462, 1971.

27. Apfeldorf, Max, Hunley, Phyllis J. and Cooper, G. David. Disci-
     plinary Problems in a Home for Older Veterans: Some Psycho-
     logical Aspects in Relation to Drinking Behavior. Geron-
     tologist, 12(2), Part I: 143-147, 1972.

28. Aquilonius, S.-M., Askmark, H., Enoksson, P., Lundberg, P.O.
     and Moström, U. Computerized tomography in severe methanol
     intoxication. British Medical Journal, 2: 929-930, 1978.

29. Archambault, A., Leroux, P. and Giroux, Y. Utilite de la pan-
     créatographie rétrograde dans le diagnostic et l'évaluation
     des pancréatites croniques éthyliques.' [Use of Retrograde
     Pancreatography in the Diagnosis and Evaluation of Alcohol-
     Induced Chronic Pancreatitis.] Vie Médicale au Canada Fran-
     çais, 6: 1068-1074, 1977.

30. Archer, Janet. Social Stability, Work Force Behavior, and Job
     Satisfaction of Alcoholic and Nonalcoholic Blue-Collar Work-
     ers. In: Alcoholism and its Treatment in Industry.
     Ed. Carl J. Schramm. Baltimore and London: The Johns Hop-
     kins University Press, 1977, pages 156-176, especially
     page 160.

31. Arieff, A.J., McCulloch, R. and Rotman, D.B. Unsuccessful Sui-
     cidal Attempts. Diseases of the Nervous System, 9: 174-179,
     1948.

32. Armor, D.J., Johnson, P., Polich, S. and Stambul, H. Trends
     in U.S. Drinking Practices: Summary Report Prepared for
     the National Institute on Alcohol Abuse and Alcoholism,
     under Contract No. ADM 281-76-0020. Santa Monica: Rand
     Corporation, 1977.

33. Arnoux, M., Mouren, P., Poinso, Y. and Chancel-Gandonnière.
     L'expertise médico-legale relative à l'alcoolisme aigu;
     considerations à propos de 240 expertises faites dans les
     Bouches-du-Rhône. [Medicolegal Expertise Concerning Acute
     Alcoholism; Considerations on 240 Reports Made in Bouches-
     du-Rhône.] Marseille Médical, 101: 13-22, 1964.

34. Arthritis and Beer Drinking. (Queries and Minor Notes.) Journal
     of the American Medical Association, 140: 1191, 1949.

35. Aschieri, G., Zamberletti, P. and Mozzicato, M. Il delirium
     tremens: Psicosi acuta da astinenza alcoolica. [Delirium
     Tremens: An Acute Psychosis of Abstinence from Alcohol.]
     Minerva Medica, 63: 4459-4469, 1972.

36. As Many as 10% of Elderly Have Alcohol Problems, White House Told.
     Alcoholism and Alcohol Education, 7(3): 5-6, 1977.

37. Atanassow, W., Tscheschmedjiev, P. and Tarnizow, I. Ist der
     plötzliche Alkoholentzug bei psychotisch gefährdeten
     Patienten medizinisch erlaubt? [Is Sudden Alcohol With-
     drawal in Patients at Risk of Psychosis Medically Permis-
     sible?] In: Papers Presented at the International Insti-
     tute on the Prevention and Treatment of Alcoholism, Dresden,
     6-10 June, 1977. Ed. E.J. Tongue and I. Moos. Lausanne:
     International Council on Alcohol and Addictions, 1977,
     pages 741-746.

38. Atkinson, Leigh, Gibson, Iris and Andrews, James. An Investi-
     gation into the Ability of Elderly Patients Continuing to
     Take Prescribed Drugs after Discharge from Hospital and
     Recommendations Concerning Improving the Situation. Geronto-
     logy, 24: 225-234, 1978.

39. Atuk, Nuzhet O., Hart, Andrew D. and Hunt, Ella H. Close Moni-
     toring Is Essential during Isoniazid Prophylaxis. Southern
     Medical Journal, 70(2): 156-159, 1977.

40. Audigier, J.C., Tuyns, A.J. and Lambert, R. Epidemiology of
     Oesophageal Cancer in France: Increasing Mortality and
     Persistent Correlation with Alcoholism. Digestion, 13:
     209-219, 1975.

41. Avrusningsstasjonen: De fleste drikker seg fra bade familie
    og arbeid; pasientenes alder varierer meloom 16 og 80.
    [Sobering-up Stations: Most People Drink Themselves Out of
    Home and Work; The Age of Patients Vary between 16 and 80.]
    Tidsskrift om Edruskaps Spørsmal, 29(3): 17-18, 1977.

42. Axelrod, L. and Vickery, A.L., Jr. Recurrent Stupor, Diabetes,
    Hypothyroidism and Liver Disease in an Elderly Woman. (Case
    Records of the Massachusetts General Hospital.) New England
    Journal of Medicine, 300: 969-976, 1979.

43. Axelrod, S., and Eisdorfer, C. Psychiatric Drug Abuse and Use
    in the Aged. Geriatrics, 25: 144-145, 148-151, 154-155, 158,
    1970.

44. Azevêdo, Eliane, Smith, Moyra, Hopkinson, D.A. and Harris, Harry.
    A Study of Possible Factors Influencing the Variation in
    Liver Alcohol Dehydrogenase Activity in Individuals of the
    "Usual" ADH Phenotype. Annals of Human Genetics, 38: 31-37,
    1974.

B

45. Bacher, F., Canoit, P., Rouquette, J., Verdeaux, G. and Verdeaux, J. Epilepsie et alcoolisme; études statistiques comparatives de critères E.E.G. [Epilepsy and Alcoholism; Comparative Statistical Studies of E.E.G. Characteristics.] Revue Neurologique, 103: 228-235, 1960.

46. Bach-i-Bach, L. Consideraciones sobre el concepto de encefalopatias alcoholicas. [Considerations on the Concept of Alcoholic Encephalopathies.] Drogalcohol, 3: 133-137, 1978.

47. Bachrach, L.L. Characteristics of Diagnosed and Missed Alcoholic Male Admissions to State and County Mental Hospitals--1972. NIMH Mental Health Statistics Note No. 124; DHEW Publication No. ADM-76158. Washington, D.C.: U.S. National Institute of Mental Health, 1976.

48. Bachrach, L.L. Educational Level of Male Admissions with Alcohol Disorders; State and County Mental Hospitals--1972. NIMH Mental Health Statistics Note No. 123; DHEW Publication No. ADM-76158. Washington, D. C.: U.S. National Institute of Mental Health, 1976.

49. Bachrach, L.L. Marital Status and Age of Male Admissions with Diagnosed Alcohol Disorders to State and County Mental Hospitals in 1972. NIMH Mental Health Statistics Note No. 120; DHEW Publ. No. ADM-76158. Washington, D.C.: U.S. National Institute of Mental Health, 1976.

50. Back, Kurt W. and Sullivan, Deborah A. Self-Image, Medicine, and Drug Use. Addictive Diseases, 3(3): 373-382, 1978.

51. Bäckman, T. Nykterhetsvård på sjukhus. [Care of Alcoholics in Hospitals.] Socialmedicinsk Tidskrift, 42: 333-336, 1965.

52. Baer, Paul E., Morin, Karen and Gaitz, Charles M. Familial Resources of Elderly Psychiatric Patients. Archives of General Psychiatry, 22(4): 343-350, 1970.

53. Bagozzi, G. Accidenti vascolari acuti cerebrali ed etilismo cronico in eta geriatrica. [Acute Cerebral Vascular Accidents and Chronic Alcoholism in the Geriatric Age.] Giornale di Gerontologia, 15: 63-73, 1967.

54. Bahn, Anita K., Anderson, Carl L. and Norman, Vivian B. Outpatient Psychiatric Clinic Services to Alcoholics, 1959. Quarterly Journal of Studies on Alcohol, 24(2): 213-226, 1963.

55. Bahn, Anita K. and Chandler, Caroline A. Alcoholism in Psychiatric Clinic Patients. Quarterly Journal of Studies on Alcohol, 22(3): 411-417, 1961.

56. Bahr, Howard M. Lifetime Affiliation Patterns of Early- and Late-Onset Heavy Drinkers on Skid Row. Quarterly Journal of Studies on Alcohol, 30: 645-656, 1969.

57. Bahr, Howard M. and Caplow, Theodore. Old Men Drunk and Sober. New York: New York University Press, 1973.

58. Bailey, Margaret B., Haberman, Paul W. and Alksne, Harold. The Epidemiology of Alcoholism in an Urban Residential Area. Quarterly Journal of Studies on Alcohol, 26: 19-40, 1965.

59. Baker, Frank, Mishara, Brian, Kastenbaum, Robert and Patterson, R. A Study of Alcohol Effects in Old Age (Phase II). Final Report to the National Institute on Alcohol Abuse and Alcoholism, under Contract #NO1-AA-3-0103, 1974. Boston: Socio-Technical Systems Associates, 1974.

60. Baker, Susan P., Robertson, Leon S. and O'Neill, Brian. Fatal Pedestrian Collisions: Driver Negligence. American Journal of Public Health, 64(4): 318-325, 1974.

61. Baker, Susan P. and Spitz, Werner U. Age Effects and Autopsy Evidence of Disease in Fatally Injured Drivers. Journal of the American Medical Association, 214(6): 1079-1088, 1970.

62. Ball, John R. Pseudocysts Ripe for Drainage. The Lancet, 1: 45, 1977.

63. Ban, T.A. Organic Problems in the Aged: Brain Syndromes and Alcoholism--Psychiatric Aspects of the Organic Brain Syndrome and Pharmacological Approaches to Treatment. Journal of Geriatric Psychiatry, 11(2): 135-159, 1978.

64. Banks, D.C. and Lecky, B.R.F. Electrolyte Disturbances in Beer Drinkers. The Lancet, 2: 559-560, 1975.

65. Barboriak, Joseph J. and Meade, Robert C. Effect of Alcohol on Gastric Emptying in Man. American Journal of Clinical Nutrition, 23(9): 1151-1153, 1970.

66. Barboriak, Joseph J., Rooney, Carol B., Leitschuh, Thomas H. and Anderson, Alfred J. Alcohol and Nutrient Intake of Elderly Men. Journal of the American Dietetic Association, 72: 493-495, 1978.

67. Barker, J.D., Jr., De Carle, D.J. and Anuras, S. Chronic Excessive Acetaminophen Use and Liver Damage. Annals of Internal Medicine, 87(3): 299-301, 1977.

68. Barker, Lewellys F. Multiple Neuritis with Macrocytic Anaemia (Both Apparently Resulting from Hypovitaminosis) in an Alcoholic Addict. Journal of Nervous and Mental Disease, 92(1): 1-4, 1940.

69. Barnes, Grace M. Alcohol Use among Older Persons: Findings from a Western New York State General Population Survey. Journal of the American Geriatrics Society, 27(6): 244-250, 1979.

70. Barnes, Grace M. and Russell, Marcia. Drinking Patterns among Adults in Western New York State: A Descriptive Analysis of the Sociodemographic Correlates of Drinking. Buffalo, New York: Research Institute on Alcoholism, 1977.

71. Barnes, Grace M. and Russell, Marcia. Drinking Patterns in Western New York State: Comparison with National Data. Journal of Studies on Alcohol, 39(7): 1148-1157, 1978.

72. Barrière, H., Stalder, J.F. and Queudet, P.Y. Le devenir clinique des porphyries cutanées tardives. [The Clinical Course of Late Cutaneous Porphyria.] Semaine des Hôpitaux de Paris, 55(1-2): 30-35, 1979.

73. Barsky, A.J., Stewart, R., Burns, B.J., Sweet, R., Regier, D. and Jacobson, A.M. Neighborhood Health Center Patients Who Use Minor Tranquilizers. International Journal of Addiction, 14: 337-354, 1979.

74. Bartecchi, Carl E., Wood, James R. and Stjernholm, Thomas. Complete Heart Block in Alcoholic Cardiomyopathy--A Potentially Reversible Process. Rocky Mountain Medical Journal, 75(5): 266-268, 1978.

75. Bartholomew, Allen A. Alcoholism and Crime. Australian and New Zealand Journal of Criminology, 1(2): 70-99, 1968.

76. Bassendine, M.F., Chadwick, R.G., Lyssiotis, T., Thomas, H.C. and Sherlock, S. Primary Liver Cell Cancer in Britain-- a Viral Aetiology? British Medical Journal, 1: 166, 1979.

77. Bauer, A. Distraneurin®¹ in der Praxis. [Distraneurin®¹ in Practice.] Zeitschrift für Allgemeinmedizin, 53(6): 342-344, 1977.

78. Baxter, A.D. Side Effects of Doxapram Infusion. European Journal of Intensive Care Medicine, 2(2): 87-88, 1976.

79. Bean, Philip. Accidental and Intentional Self-Poisoning in the Over 60 Age Group. Gerontological Clinician, 15: 259-267, 1973.

80. Beattie, B.L. and Sellers, E.M. Psychoactive Drug Use in the Elderly: The Pharmacokinetics. Psychosomatics, 20(7): 474-479, 1979.

81. Becker, Paul W. and Cesar, Joseph A. Use of Beer in Geriatric Psychiatric Patient Groups. Psychological Reports, 33: 182, 1973.

82. Becker, Paul W. and Conn, S. Hall. Beer and Social Therapy Treatment with Geriatric Psychiatric Patient Groups. Addictive Diseases, 3(3): 429-436, 1978.

83. Bedate-Villar, J. and Arocas-Estelles, A. Revision de los alcoholicos tratados por primera vez durante 1977 en el Hospital Psiquiatrico de Betera (Valencia). [Evaluation of the Alcoholics Who Were First-Time Admissions during 1977 at the Betera (Valencia) Psychiatric Hospital.] Drogalcohol, 3: 121-131, 1978.

84. Beerman, B., Biörck, G. and Groschinsky-Grind, M. Läkemedels-biverkningar och intoxikationer somorsak till intagning på invärtesmedicinsk klinik. [Adverse Drug Reactions and Poisonings as Causes for Admission to a Medical Clinic.] Läkartidningen, 75: 958-960, 1978.

85 Beevers, D.G. Alcohol and Hypertension. The Lancet, 2(8029): 114-115, 1977.

86. Bélanger, M., St-Hilaire, D. and Lessard, A. Recherches sur deux nouveaux tests de dépistage précoce de la cirrhose alcoolique. [Research on Two New Tests for Early Detection of Alcoholic Cirrhosis.] Union Médicale du Canada, 103: 1557-1564, 1974.

87. Bell, R.G. Clinical Orientation to Alcoholism. Industrial Medicine and Surgery, 21(6): 251-260, 1952.

88. Bello, Sergio and Salinas, M. Judith. Evaluacion de un programma de prevencion secundaria del alcoholismo. [Evaluation of a Program for Secondary Prevention of Alcoholism.] Revista Médica Chile, 106(8): 636-640, 1978.

89. Bender, A. Douglas. Geriatric Pharmacology: Age and Its Influence on Drug Action in Adults. Drug Information Bulletin, 3: 153-158, 1969.

90. Bender, A. Douglas. Pharmacologic Aspects of Aging: A Survey
    of the Effect of Increasing Age on Drug Activity in Adults.
    Journal of the American Geriatrics Society, 12(2): 114-134,
    1964.

91. Béraud, C., Amouretti, M., Boisseau, C. and Couzigou, P. Le
    pronostic des cirrhoses alcooliques. [Prognosis in Alco-
    holic Cirrhosis.] Revue du Praticien, 26: 3665-3669, 1976.

92. Beregi, E., Lengyel, E. and Biró, J. Autoantibodies in Aged
    Individuals. Aktuelle Gerontologie, 8(2): 77-80, 1978.

93. Bergeron, M. and Hanus, M. Les etats dementiels réversibles.
    [Reversible Demential States.] Annales Médico-Psycho-
    logiques, 122: 529-553, 1964.

94. Berglin, Carl-Gustaf. Sjukdom och invaliditet hos 67 alko-
    holister observerade i 19 ar. [Health Study of 67 Alco-
    holics Observed for Nineteen Years in a Nursing Home.]
    Läkartidningen, 71(38): 3522-3523, 1974.

95. Berglin, Carl-Gustaf and Rosengren, Enoch. Arbetsprestationer
    och pensionering hos 868 alkoholister. [Work Performance
    of 868 Alcoholics in a Home for Pensioners.] Läkartid-
    ningen, 71(38): 3520-3521, 1974.

96. Berglund, Mats, Gustafson, L., Hagberg, B., Ingvar, David H.,
    Nilsson, L., Risberg, J. and Sonesson, B. Cerebral Dys-
    function in Alcoholism and Presenile Dementia: A Compari-
    son of Two Groups of Patients with Similar Reduction of
    the Cerebral Blood Flow. Acta Psychiatrica Scandinavica,
    55: 391-398, 1977.

97. Berglund, Mats and Ingvar, David H. Cerebral Blood Flow and
    Its Regional Distribution in Alcoholism and in Korsakoff's
    Psychosis. Journal of Studies on Alcohol, 37(5): 586-597,
    1976.

98. Berkman, L.F. and Syme, S.L. Social Networks, Host Resistance,
    and Mortality: A Nine-Year Follow-Up of Alameda County
    Residents. American Journal of Epidemiology, 109(2):
    186-204, 1979.

99. Bertera, J.H. and Parsons, O.A. Impaired Visual Search in
    Alcoholics. Alcoholism: Clinical and Experimental Re-
    search, 2: 9-14, 1978.

100. Bertrand, J., Thomas, J. and Metman, E.H. Maladie de Dupuytren
     et érythrose palmaire au cours des cirrhoses éthyliques.
     [Dupuytren's Contracture and Palmar Erythema in Alcoholic
     Cirrhosis.] Semaine des Hôpitaux de Paris, 53(7): 407-412,
     1977.

101. Bircher, Johannes, Küpfer, Adrian, Gikalov, Iva and Preišig,
      Rudolf. Aminopyrine Demethylation Measured by Breath
      Analysis in Cirrhosis. Clinical Pharmacology and Thera-
      peutics, 20(4): 484-492, 1976.

102. Birkett, D. J., Graham, G.G., Chinwah, P.M., Wade, D.N. and
      Hickie, J.B. Multiple Drug Interactions with Phenytoin.
      Medical Journal of Australia, 2: 467-468, 1977.

103. Bischof, H.L. Zur Pathogenese des Alkoholdelirs: Dargestellt
      Aufgrund von Beobachtungen an 209 Fällen. [The Pathogenesis
      of Alcoholic Delirium: Based on Observations in 209 Cases.]
      Der Nervenarzt, 40(7): 318-325, 1969.

104. Bischoff, A. Die alkoholische Polyneuropathie; klinische,
      ultrastrukturelle und pathogenetische Aspekte. [Alcoholic
      Polyneuropathy; Clinical, Ultrastructural and Pathogenic
      Aspects.] Deutsche Medizinische Wochenschrift, 96: 317-322,
      1971.

105. Bjerver, K. A Long-Term Study on Morbidity among Alcoholics in
      Stockholm. Protialkoholicky Obzor, 6: 6-11, 1971.

106. Bjurulf, P., Sternby, N.H., and Wistedt, B. Definitions of
      Alcoholism: Relevance of Liver Disease and Temperance
      Board Registrations in Sweden. Quarterly Journal of Studies
      on Alcohol, 32(2): 393-405, 1971.

107. Black, Arthur L. Altering Behavior of Geriatric Patients with
      Beer. Northwest Medicine, 68(5): 453-456, 1969.

108. Blane, H.T. Acculturation and Drinking in an Italian American
      Community. Journal of Studies on Alcohol, 38(7): 1324-1346,
      1977.

109. Blaney, Roger and Radford, Inge S. The Prevalence of Alcoholism
      in an Irish Town. Quarterly Journal of Studies on Alcohol,
      34: 1255-1269, 1973.

110. Blaney, Roger, Radford, Inge S. and Mackenzie, G. A Belfast
      Study of the Prediction of Outcome in the Treatment of Alco-
      holism. British Journal of Addiction, 70: 41-50, 1975.

111. Blose, Irvin L. The Relationship of Alcohol to Aging and the
      Elderly. Alcoholism, 2(1): 17-21, 1978.

112. Blum, J. and Levine, J. Maturity, Depression, and Life Events
      in Middle-Aged Alcoholics. Addictive Behavior, 1: 37-45,
      1975.

113. Blum, Richard H. Users of Approved Drugs. In: Students and
      Drugs: College and High School Observations. Ed. Rich-
      ard H. Blum. Vol. 2. San Francisco: Jolley-Bass, 1970,
      pages 111-131.

114. Blumberg, Leonard U., Shipley, Thomas E., Jr., and Barsky,
      Stephen F. Liquor and Poverty: Skid Row as a Human Con-
      dition. (Monographs of the Rutgers Center of Alcohol Studies,
      No. 13.) New Brunswick, New Jersey: Publications Division,
      Rutgers Center of Alcohol Studies, 1978, especially pages 107,
      134-136, 173.

115. Blumberg, Leonard, Shipley, Thomas E., Jr., Shandler, Irving W.
      and Niebuhr, Herman. The Development, Major Goals and
      Strategies of a Skid Row Program: Philadelphia. Quarterly
      Journal of Studies on Alcohol, 27(2): 242-258, 1966.

116. Blusewicz, Matthew J., Dustman, Robert E., Schenkenberg, Thomas
      and Beck, Edward C. Neuropsychological Correlates of Chronic
      Alcoholism and Aging. The Journal of Nervous and Mental
      Disease, 165(5): 348-355, 1977.

117. Blusewicz, Matthew J., Schenkenberg, Thomas, Dustman, Robert E.
      and Beck, Edward C. WAIS Performance in Young Normal,
      Young Alcoholic, and Elderly Normal Groups: An Evaluation
      of Organicity and Mental Aging Indices. Journal of Clinical
      Psychology, 33(4): 1149-1153, 1977.

118. Bock, Jorgen. Liver Cirrhosis in the Aged. Journal of Geron-
      tology, 3: 111-118, 1948.

119. Bock, O.A.A. Alcohol, Aspirin, Depression, Smoking, Stress and
      the Patient with a Gastric Ulcer. South African Medical
      Journal, 50: 293-297, 1976.

120. Bohrod, Milton G. Primary Degeneration of the Corpus Callosum
      (Marchiafava's Disease): Report of the Second American
      Case. Archives of Neurology and Psychiatry, 47: 465-473,
      1942.

121. Boles, R.S., Crew, R.S. and Dunbar, W. "Alcoholic Cirrhosis."
      Journal of the American Medical Association, 134: 670-673,
      678-679, 1947.

122. Bonfiglio, G. Alcoholism in Italy. British Journal of Addic-
      tion, 59: 3-12, 1963.

123. Borg, Stefan. Homeless Men: A Clinical and Social Study with
      Special Reference to Alcohol Abuse. Acta Psychiatrica
      Scandinavica (Supplementum), 276, 11-90, 1978.

124. Borowsky, S.A., Hasse, A., Wiedlin, R. and Lott, E. Dental In-
      fection in a Cirrhotic Patient; Source of Recurrent Sepsis.
      Gastroenterology, 76: 836-839, 1979.

125. Botteghelli, R. Danno iatrogenico in pazienti alcoolisti cronici
      sottoposti a trattamento divezzante con tetraetiltiuram-
      disulfuro. [Iatrogenic Damage in Chronic Alcoholics after
      Withdrawal Treatment with Tetraethylthiuram Disulfide.]
      Minerva Medica, 62: 741-742, 1971.

126. Bottinelli, R.W. Drinking Patterns of the Elderly Single Room
     Occupancy Hotel Resident. Ph.D. Dissertation. The Medical
     College of Pennsylvania, 1978. (University Microfilms
     No. 78-15851.)

127. Botwinick, Jack. Aging and Behavior: A Comprehensive Integra-
     tion of Research Findings. 2nd ed. New York: Springer
     Publishing Co. 1978.

128. Bourne, Peter G. Drug Abuse in the Aging. Perspectives on
     Aging, 2(3): 18-20, 1973.

129. Bozzetti, Louis P. and MacMurray, James P. Drug Misuse among
     the Elderly: A Hidden Menace. Psychiatric Annals, 7(3):
     155-161, 1977.

130. Braucht, G.N., Kirby, M.W. and Berry, G.J. Psychosocial Cor-
     relates of Empirical Types of Multiple Drug Abusers.
     Journal of Consulting and Clinical Psychology, 46: 1463-
     1475, 1978.

131. Brenner, Berthold. Alcoholism and Fatal Accidents. Quarterly
     Journal of Studies on Alcohol, 28(3): 517-528, 1967.

132. Brickner, Philip W. and Kaufman, Arthur. Case Finding of Heart
     Disease in Homeless Men. Bulletin of the New York Academy
     of Medicine, 49(6): 475-484, 1973.

133. Bridger, G.P. and Reay-Young, P. Laryngeal Cancer and Smoking.
     Medical Journal of Australia, 63: 293-294, 1976.

134. Briganti, Frank J. Side Effects of Drugs Used by the Elderly.
     In: Drugs and the Elderly. Ed. Richard H. Davis and
     William K. Smith. Los Angeles, California: The Ethel Per-
     cy Andrus Gerontology Center, University of Southern Cali-
     fornia Press, 1973, pages 25-32.

135. Brisolara, Ashton. The Alcoholic Employee: A Handbook of Use-
     ful Guidelines. New York: Human Sciences Press, 1979,
     especially page 56.

136. Broadhurst, N.A. and Smith, K. A South Australian Survey on
     Attitudes to Cigarettes and Beer. Australian Journal of
     Alcoholism and Drug Dependence, 3: 26-27, 1976.

137. Brodanová, M., Hoenig, V., Kordač, V. and Skála, J. Resorpce
     železa z travicího traktu u zdravých, alkoholiků a nemocných
     s jaterní cirhózou. [Iron Absorption from the Digestive
     Tract in Healthy Persons, in Alcoholics and in Patients with
     Liver Cirrhosis.] Časopis Lekaru Čeckych, 108: 1382-1385,
     1969.

138. Brooks, Benjamin Rix and Adams, Raymond D. Cerebrospinal Fluid
      Acid-Base and Lactate Changes after Seizures in Unanesthe-
      tized Man. II. Alcohol Withdrawal Seizures. Neurology,
      25: 943-948, 1975.

139. Brooks, Harlow. The Use of Alcohol in the Circulatory Defects
      of Old Age. Medical Journal and Record, 127(4): 199-206,
      1928.

140. Bross, I.D.J. and Coombs, J. Early Onset of Oral Cancer among
      Women Who Drink and Smoke. Oncology, 33(3): 136-139, 1976.

141. Brown, J.B. Platelet Mao and Alcoholism. American Journal of
      Psychiatry, 134(2): 206-207, 1977.

142. Browne-Mayers, A.N., Seelye, E.E. and Sillman, L. Psychosocial
      Study of Hospitalized Middle-Class Alcoholic Women. Annals
      of the New York Academy of Sciences, 273: 593-604, 1976.

143. Brun, D., Moorjani, S., Lupien, P.-J. and Bélanger, G. Chylo-
      micronémie induite par l'alcool dans l'hyperlipoprotéinémie
      de type IV. [Alcohol-Induced Chylomicronemia in Type IV
      Hyperlipoproteinemia.] Union Médicale du Canada, 102: 1710-
      1714, 1973.

144. Buehrer, O.A. Über 204 Fälle von Delirium tremens. [Regarding
      204 Cases of Delirium Tremens.] Münchener Medizinische
      Wochenschrift, 106, 1016, 1964.

145. Buess, H.J., Mihatsch, M.J., Wunderlich, P. and Berger, W. Lak-
      tatazidose bei Diabetes mellitus. [Lactic Acidosis in Dia-
      betes Mellitus.] Praxis, 65(14): 406-413, 1976.

146. Buge, A., Escourolle, R., Tempier, P., Hauw, J.-J. and Rancur-
      el, G. Tuberculose cerebrale: 3 observations anatomo-
      cliniques. [Cerebral Tuberculosis: Three Clinicopatholog-
      ical Cases.] Nouvelle Presse Médicale, 7(16): 1377-1380,
      1978.

147. Bürkle, P.A. and Mallach, H.J. Statische Untersuchungen über den
      Einfluss von Lebensalter, Körperläge und -gewicht auf den
      Diagnosegrad bei Personen mit hohen Blutalkoholwerten.
      [Statistical Studies regarding the Effect of Age, Height and
      Weight on the Diagnosis of Persons with a High Blood Alcohol
      Content.] Blutalkohol, 5: 355-358, 1968.

148. Burns, M., Daily, J.M. and Moskowitz, H. Drinking Practices and
      Problems of Urban American Indians in Los Angeles. Part I.
      Study Description and Findings. Preliminary Report. Santa
      Monica, California: Planning Analysis and Research Insti-
      tute, 1974.

149. Burrill, Roger H., McCourt, James F. and Cutter, Henry S.G. Beer:
      A Social Facilitator for PMI Patients? Gerontologist, 14(5):
      430-431, 1974.

150. Burville, P. Consecutive Psychogeriatric Admissions to Psychia-
     tric and Geriatric Hospitals. Geriatrics, 26: 156-168, 1971.

151. Busche, P., Marg, E. and Knittel, H.-J. Zum Problem des chron-
     ischen Alkoholismus; vergleichenede Untersuchung der wegen
     chronischen Alkoholmissbrauches und Delirium tremens auf-
     genommen männlichen Patienten der Nervenklinik Neuruppin.
     [On the Problem of Chronic Alcoholism; Comparable Examination
     of the Male Patients Admitted to the Neuruppin Neurological
     Clinic on Account of Chronic Alcohol Misuse and Delirium
     Tremens.] Psychiatrie, Neurologie und Medizinische Psycho-
     logie, 22: 418-423, 1970.

152. Buser, E.R. Antabuspsychose. [Antabuse Psychosis.] Ars Medici,
     42: 555, 1952.

153. Bushinsky, D.A. and Gennari, F.J. Life-Threatening Hyperkalemia
     Induced by Arginine. Annals of Internal Medicine, 89(5):
     632-634, 1978.

154. Butler, Frank S. Alcoholism: Control of the Uncontrolled Alco-
     holic. Journal of the American Geriatrics Society, 15(9):
     848-851, 1967.

155. Butler, R.N. Clinical Psychiatry in Late Life. In: Clinical
     Geriatrics. Ed. I. Rossman. Philadelphia, Pennsylvania:
     J.B. Lippincott, 1971, pages 439-459.

156. Butler, R.N. Why Survive? Being Old in America. New York:
     Harper and Row, 1975.

157. Butler, R.N. and Lewis, M.I. Sex after Sixty: A Guide for Men
     and Women for Their Later Years. New York: Harper and Row,
     1976.

158. Butler, R.N. and Lewis, M.I. Special Concerns--Racism, Sexism,
     Retirement, Crime, Alcoholism, and Sexuality. In: Aging
     and Mental Health: Positive Psychosocial Approaches.
     St. Louis, Missouri: C.V. Mosby and Co., 1973 (2nd ed.,
     1977), Chapter 6, pages 83-105.

159. Butters, Nelson, Cermak, Laird S., Montgomery, Kathleen and
     Adinolfi, Allen. Some Comparisons of the Memory and Visuo-
     perceptive Deficits of Chronic Alcoholics and Patients with
     Korsakoff's Disease. Alcoholism: Clinical and Experimental
     Research, 1(1): 73-80, 1977.

160. Butters, Nelson and Grady, M. Effect of Predistractor Delays
     on the Short-Term Memory Performance of Patients with
     Korsakoff's and Huntington's Disease. Neuropsychologia,
     15: 701-706, 1977.

161. Butters, Nelson, Tarlow, S., Cermak, Laird and Sax, D. A Com-
     parison of the Information Processing Deficits of Patients
     with Huntington's Chorea and Korsakoff's Syndrome. Cortex,
     12: 134-144, 1976.

C

162. Cahalan, Don. Drinking Practices and Problems; Research Perspectives on Remedial Measures. Public Affairs Report, 14(2): 1-6, 1973.

163. Cahalan, Don. Problem Drinkers: A National Survey. San Francisco, California: Jossey-Bass, 1970.

164. Cahalan, Don and Cisin, Ira H. American Drinking Practices: Summary of Findings from a National Probability Sample. I. Extent of Drinking by Population Subgroups. Quarterly Journal of Studies on Alcohol, 29: 130-151, 1968.

165. Cahalan, Don and Cisin, Ira H. American Drinking Practices: Summary of Findings from a National Probability Sample. II. Measurement of Massed Versus Spaced Drinking. Quarterly Journal of Studies on Alcoholism, 29(3): 642-656, 1968.

166. Cahalan, Don, Cisin, Ira H. and Crossley, Helen M. American Drinking Practices: A National Survey of Drinking Behavior and Attitudes. Monograph No. 6. New Brunswick, New Jersey: Rutgers Center of Alcohol Studies, 1969.

167. Cahalan, Don, Cisin, Ira H. and Crossley, Helen M. American Drinking Practices: A National Survey of Behavior and Attitudes Related to Alcoholic Beverages. Washington, D.C.: The George Washington University Social Research Group, Report No. 3, 1967.

168. Cahalan, Don and Room, Robin. Problem Drinking among American Men. Monograph No. 7. New Brunswick, New Jersey: Rutgers Center of Alcohol Studies, 1974.

169. Callaway, J. Lamar and Tate, William E. Toxic Epidermal Necrolysis Caused by "Gin and Tonic." Archiv für Dermatologische Forschung, 109: 909, 1974.

170. Cameron, D. Ewen. The Elderly Alcoholic. In: Second Symposium
     on the Clinical Problems of Advancing Years. Philadelphia,
     Pennsylvania: Smith, Kline, and French Laboratories, 1951,
     pages 11-13.

171. Capel, William C. and Peppers, Larry G. The Aging Addict: A
     Longitudinal Study of Known Abusers. Addictive Diseases,
     3(3): 389-403, 1978.

172. Caplan, L.R. and Schoene, W.C. Clinical Features of Subcortical
     Arteriosclerotic Encephalopathy (Binswanger Disease).
     Neurology, 28: 1206-1215, 1978.

173. Carlen, P.L., Wortzman, G., Holgate, R.C., Wilkinson, D.A. and
     Rankin, J.G. Reversible Cerebral Atrophy in Recently Ab-
     stinent Chronic Alcoholics Measured by Computed Tomography
     Scans. Science, 200: 1076-1078, 1978.

174. Carlsson, Carl, Dencker, Sven J., Grimby, Gunnar and Tichý, Jiří.
     Muscle Weakness and Neurological Disorders in Alcoholics.
     Quarterly Journal of Studies on Alcohol, 30(3): 585-591,
     1969.

175. Carney, M.W.P. Serum Folate and Cyanocobalamin in Alcoholics.
     Quarterly Journal of Studies on Alcohol, 31(4): 816-822,
     1970.

176. Carp, Frances M. and Katacka, Eunice. Health Care Problems of
     the Elderly of San Francisco's Chinatown. DHEW Publication
     No. AA-4-70-087, 1976.

177. Carrieri, F. Alcoolismo e invalidità pensionabile. [Alcoholism
     and Disability Compensation.] Rivista Italiana di Previ-
     denza Sociale, 3: 466, 1971.

178. Carroll, Paul J. The Social Hour for Geropsychiatric Patients.
     Journal of the American Geriatrics Society, 26(1): 32-35,
     1978.

179. Carruth, Bruce. Alcoholism and Problem Drinking among Older
     Persons: Lifestyles, Drinking Practices and Drinking
     Problems of Older Alcoholics. Paper presented at the
     National Council on Alcoholism Annual Meetings, April 28-
     May 3, 1974, Denver, Colorado. New Brunswick, New Jersey:
     Rutgers Center of Alcohol Studies Research supported by
     Grant #PHS-SRS-93-P-75146/2-02, Administration on Aging,
     Department of Health, Education, and Welfare.

180. Carruth, Bruce, Williams, Erma Polly, Mysak, Patricia and Bou-
     dreaux, Louis, Jr. Alcoholism and Problem Drinking among
     Older Persons: Community Care Providers and the Older Prob-
     lem Drinker. A Policy and Planning Statement. In: Selected
     Papers Presented at the General Session--Twenty-fourth Annual
     Meeting of the Alcohol and Drug Problems Association of North
     America, Minneapolis, Minnesota, 23-28 September, 1973. Wash-
     ington, D.C.: Alcohol and Drug Problems Association, 1973.

181. Carruth, Bruce, Williams, Erma Polly, Mysak, Patricia, and Boudreaux, Louis, Jr. Community Care Providers and the Older Problem Drinker. Grassroots (July Supplement): 1-5, 1975.

182. Carruth, Bruce, Williams, Erma Polly, Mysak, Patricia, Boudreaux, Louis, Jr., Hyman, Merton M., Maxwell, Milton, Jones, Robert W. and Roth, Barbara. Alcoholism and Problem Drinking among Older Persons. Final Report of Study, 1972-1973, prepared under Grant No. PHS-SRS-93-P-75146/2-02 for the Administration on Aging, U.S. Department of Health, Education, and Welfare. New Brunswick, New Jersey: Rutgers Center of Alcohol Studies, Rutgers University, 1973; and Springfield, Virginia: NTIS, 1973.

183. Carter, A.B. The Neurologic Aspects of Aging. In: Clinical Geriatrics. Ed. I. Rossman. Philadelphia: J.B. Lippincott, 1971, pages 123-141.

184. Casale, G. and Guaita, A. Alcool, lipidi ematici ed età avanzata. [Alcohol, Blood Lipids, and Old Age.] Minerva Medica, 69: 1015-1018, 1978.

185. Castelli, W.P., Gordon, T., Hjortland, M.C., Kagan, A., Doyle, J.T., Hames, C.G., Hulley, S.B. and Zukel, W.J. Alcohol and Blood Lipids; the Cooperative Lipoprotein Phenotyping Study. The Lancet, 2: 153-155, 1977.

186. Cavaliēri, Ugo. Adattamento dell'anziano ed alcoolismo. [Adaptation in the Elderly and Alcoholism.] Longevità, 5: 199-200, 1957.

187. Cavaliēri, Ugo. Alcool e vecchiaia; pregiudizi e nozioni. [Alcohol and Old Age; Prejudices and Information.] Giornale di Gerontologia, 15(1): 37-43, 1967.

188. Cavaliēri, Ugo. Alcoolismo e vecchiaia. [Alcoholism and Old Age.] Longevità, 4(2-3): 45-48, 1954.

189. Cavaliēri, Ugo. Aspects of Clinical Pathology; Senile Mental Deterioration. Minerva Medica, 52, 2632-2642, 1961.

190. Cavaliēri, Ugo. L'alcool: Un fattore di "controrischio" e di longevita? [Alcohol: Is It a Risk-Counteracting Factor of Longevity?] Rassegna Clinico-Scientifica, 53: 159-160, 1977.

191. Cavaliēri, Ugo and Quadri, A. Sul comportamento dell'organismo senile sotto l'anzione dell'alcool. Altre ricerche. [On the Behavior of the Aged Body under the Influence of Alcohol. Further Research.] Giornale di Gerontologia, 7: 559-571, 1959.

192. Cavaliēri, Ugo, Quadri, A. and Tammaro, A.E. Alcool e catecol-
     amine nell'organismo senile; prove con noradrenalina. [Alco-
     hol and Catecholamines in the Aged Body; Tests with Noradren-
     aline.] Minerva Medica, 53: 1150-1155, 1962.

193. Cavaliēri, Ugo, Quadri, A. and Tammaro, A.E. Cold pressor test
     ed alcool nell'organismo senile. [Cold Pressor Test and
     Alcohol in the Aged Body.] Minerva Medica, 54: 2654-2655,
     1963.

194. Cavaliēri, Ugo, Quadri, A. and Tammaro, A.E. Fattore chiarifi-
     cante ed alcool nell'organismo senile. [The Clearing Factor
     and Alcohol in the Aged Body.] Giornale di Gerontologia, 7:
     719-724, 1959.

195. Cavaliēri, Ugo, Quadri, A. and Tammaro, A.E. Iperlipemia da
     pasto grasso ed alcool nell'organismo senile. [Hyperlipemia
     Induced by a Fatty Meal and Alcohol in the Aged Body.]
     Minerva Medica, 53: 1143-1146, 1962.

196. Cavaliēri, Ugo., Quadri, A. and Tammaro, A.E. Iperlipemia da
     pasto grasso ed alcool nell'organismo senile; altre ricerche.
     [Hyperlipemia Induced by a Fatty Meal and Alcohol in the
     Aged Body; Further Research.] Minerva Medica, 53: 1146-1150,
     1962.

197. Cavaliēri, Ugo, Quadri, A. and Tammaro, A.E. Su una azione
     reserpino-simile dell'alcool nell'organismo senile. [On a
     Reserpine-like Action of Alcohol in the Aged Body.] Gior-
     nale di Gerontologia, 10: 1355-1359, 1962.

198. Cavaliēri, Ugo, Quadri, A. and Tammaro, A.E. Test all'angioten-
     sina ed alcool nell'organismo senile. [Angiotensin Test and
     Alcohol in the Aged Body.] Minerva Medica, 54: 2654-2655,
     1963.

199. Cavaliēri, Ugo, Quadri, A. and Tammaro, A.E. Ulteriori contributi
     allo studio dei rapporti tra alcool e organismo senile.
     [Further Contribution to the Study of the Reports Involving
     Alcohol and the Aged Body.] Minerva Medica, 52: 1390-1396,
     1961.

200. Cavaliēri, Ugo and Tammaro, A.E. Su alcuni effetti dell'alcool
     etilico, in rapporto a condizioni di fisiopatalogia vascolare
     senile. [Some Effects of Ethyl Alcohol, in Relation to the
     Condition of Senile Vascular Physiopathology.] Giornale
     dell'Arteriosclerosi, 1: 104, 1964.

201. Cavaliēri, Ugo, Tammaro, A.E. and Quadri, A. Influenza dell'al-
     cool etilico sulle modificazioni lipidemiche da pasto grasso
     in soggetti anziani. [Influence of Ethyl Alcohol on Lipid
     Modifications by a Fatty Meal in Elderly Subjects.] Gior-
     nale di Gerontologia, 13: 1079, 1965.

202. Cavaliéri, Ugo, Tammaro, A.E. and Quadri, A. Ricenti richerche
     sul comportamento dell'alcool etilico nell'organismo senile.
     [Recent Research in the Action of Ethyl Alcohol in the Aged
     Body.] Minerva Medica, 56: 2213-2215, 1965.

203. Cavaliéri, Ugo, Tammaro, A.E. and Quadri, A. Su alcuni rapporti
     tra nialamide, reserpina ed alcool nell'organismo senile.
     [On Some Relations between Nialamide, Reserpine and Alcohol
     in the Aged Body.] Giornale di Gerontologia, 12: 623-628,
     1964.

204. Cavaliéri, Ugo, Tammaro, A.E. and Quadri, A. Su una anzione
     ipoglicemizzante dell'alcool; uno studio su soggetti an-
     ziani. [Hypoglycemic Action of Ethyl Alcohol; A Study in
     Elderly Subjects.] Minerva Medica, 54: 2652-2654, 1963.

205. Cavaliéri, Ugo, Tammaro, A.E., Quadri, A. and Baldoli, C. In-
     fluenza dell'alcool etilico sulle alterazioni elettro cardio-
     grafiche da pasto grasso nell'organismo senile. [Effect in
     the Aged Body of Ethyl Alcohol on Electrocardiograph Alter-
     ations from a Fatty Meal.] Minerva Medica, 56: 2218-2220,
     1965.

206. Cavaliéri, Ugo, Tammaro, A.E., Quadri, A. and Baldoli, C. Su al-
     cuni aspetti di farmacologia clinico-geriatrica dell'alcool
     etilico. [Some Aspects of the Clinico-Geriatric Pharmacology
     of Ethyl Alcohol.] Atti del Simposio Internazionale di
     Zooteonia, 1965.

207. Cecil, Russell L. Old Age and the Vices. Journal of the American
     Geriatrics Society, 1: 604-608, 1953.

208. Cederlof, R., Friberg, L. and Lundman, T. The Interactions of
     Smoking, Environment and Heredity and Their Implications for
     Disease Etiology: A Report of Epidemiological Studies on
     the Swedish Twin Registries. Acta Medica Scandinavica, Sup-
     plementum 612: 1-128, 1977.

209. Celentano, D.D. and McQueen, D.V. Comparison of Alcoholism
     Prevalence Rates Obtained by Survey and Indirect Estimators.
     Journal of Studies on Alcohol, 39(3): 420-434, 1978.

210. Cermak, Laird S. and Reale, L. Depth of Processing and Retention
     of Words by Alcoholic Korsakoff Patients. Journal of Ex-
     perimental Psychology: Learning and Memory, 4: 165-174,
     1978.

211. Cermak, Laird S., Reale, L., and Baker, E. Alcoholic Korsakoff
     Patients' Retrieval from Semantic Memory. Brain and Lan-
     guage, 5: 215-226, 1978.

212. Cermak, Laird S. and Ryback, Ralph S. Recovery of Verbal Short-
     Term Memory in Alcoholics. Journal of Studies on Alcohol,
     37(1): 46-52, 1976.

213. Chafetz, Morris. Why Drinking Can Be Good for You. New York: Stein and Day, 1976, especially page 53.

214. Chambers, C.D. and Griffey, M.S. Use of Legal Substances within the General Population: The Sex and Age Variables. Addictive Diseases, 2: 7-19, 1975.

215. Chambers, Francis T., Jr. and Appel, Kenneth E. The Drinker's Addiction: Its Nature and Practical Treatment. Springfield, Illinois: Charles C. Thomas, 1968, especially pages 25-26.

216. Chandler, Jane, Hensman, Celia and Edwards, Griffith. Determinants of What Happens to Alcoholics. Quarterly Journal of Studies on Alcohol, 32(2): 349-363, 1971.

217. Chapman, R.F. and Smith, J.W. Peripheral Neuropathy and Electrical Aversion Treatment of Alcoholism. Behavior Therapy, 3: 469-471, 1972.

218. Chaput, J.-C., Petite, J.-P., Gueroult, N., Buffet, C., Regensberg, M. and Etienne, J.-P. La fibroscopie d'urgence dans les hémorragies digestives des cirrhoses; à propos de 100 cas. [Emergency Fibroscopy in Digestive Hemorrhage in Cirrhosis; Concerning 100 Cases.] Nouvelle Presse Médicale, 3: 1227-1230, 1974.

219. Chen, K.K. and Robbins, E. Brown. Influence of Age of Mice on the Toxicity of Alcohol. Journal of the American Pharmacological Association, 33: 62-63, 1944.

220. Chesrow, Eugene J., Kaplitz, Sherman E., Levine, Jacob M., Musci, Joseph P. and Sabatini, Raoul. The Use of Chlordiazepoxide (Librium) in the Alcoholic Patient: A Clinical Study of Forty Cases. Journal of the American Geriatrics Society, 10: 264-269, 1962.

221. Chien, Ching-Piao. Psychiatric Treatment for Geriatric Patients: "Pub" or Drug? American Journal of Psychiatry, 127(8): 1070-1075, 1971.

222. Chien, Ching-Piao, Stotsky, Bernard A. and Cole, Jonathan O. Psychiatric Treatment for Nursing Home Patients: Drug, Alcohol, and Milieu. American Journal of Psychiatry, 130(5): 543-548, 1973.

223. Chien, Ching-Piao, Townsend, Ernest J. and Ross-Townsend, Anita. Substance Use and Abuse among the Community Elderly: The Medical Aspect. Addictive Diseases, 3(3): 357-372, 1978.

224. Chiles, J.A. A Practical Therapeutic Use of the Telephone. American Journal of Psychiatry, 131: 1030-1031, 1974.

225. Chilvers, Clair, Fraser, Patricia, and Beral, Valerie. Alcohol and Oesophageal Cancer: An Assessment of the Evidence from Routinely Collected Data. Journal of Epidemiology and Community Health, 33(2): 127-133, 1979.

226. Christmas, June J. The Delivery of Alcoholism Services: Meeting
     Whose Needs? Paper presented at the Seminar on Alcoholism
     Treatment in Prepaid Group Practice Health Maintenance
     Organizations. Boston, Massachusetts, 25 February 1977.

227. Chronic Urticaria Regressing with Intake of Alcoholic Beverages.
     (Questions and Answers.) Journal of the American Medical
     Association, 237: 1377, 1977.

228. Chu, George. Drinking Patterns and Attitudes of Rooming-House
     Chinese in San Francisco. Quarterly Journal of Studies
     on Alcohol (Supplement No. 6): 58-68, 1972.

229. Cielo, R., Olivieri, P.G. and Valmachino, V.G. Le anemie
     nell'etilismo cronico. [Anemias in Chronic Ethylism.]
     Minerva Medica, 61: 243-247, 1970.

230. Ciompi, L. Geronto-Psychiatric Literature in the Postwar Period:
     A Review of the Literature to January 1, 1965. Public
     Health Service Publication No. 1811. Chevy Chase, Maryland:
     U.S. Department of Health, Education, and Welfare, NIMH,
     1969, pages 16-17. (Also appeared as: Gerontopsychiatrische
     Literatur der Nachkriegszeit; ein Sammelreferat. [Postwar
     Gerontopsychiatric Literature; a Review.] Fortschritte der
     Neurologie, Psychiatrie und ihrer Grenzgebiete, 34: 49-159,
     1966.)

231. Ciompi, L. Über Altersveränderungen vorbestehender psychischer
     Krankheiten (speciell Alkoholismus) und ihre Beziehung zur
     Therapie. [On the Change with Age of a Particular Psycho-
     logical Disorder (Alcoholism) and its Relation to Therapy.]
     Aktuelle Gerontologie, 2(3): 271-277, 1972.

232. Ciompi, L. and Eisert, M. Etudes catamnestiques de longue durée
     sur le vieillissement des alcooliques. [Retrospective Long-
     Term Studies on the Health Status of Alcoholics in Old Age.]
     Social Psychiatry, 6(3): 129-151, 1971.

233. Ciompi, L. and Eisert, M. Mortalité et causes de décès chez les
     alcooliques. [Mortality and Causes of Death in Alcoholics.]
     Social Psychiatry, 4(4): 159-168, 1969.

234. Cisin, Ira H. Summary of a Survey on American Drinking Practices.
     [See Entry #166.] Presented at the Annual Meeting of the
     North American Association of Alcoholism Programs, Albuquer-
     que, New Mexico, October 11, 1966. In: U.S. National Insti-
     tute of Mental Health, National Clearinghouse for Mental
     Health Information, Mental Health Program Reports, No. 3.

235. Cisin, Ira H. and Cahalan, Don. Comparison of Abstainers and
     Heavy Drinkers in a National Survey. Psychiatric Research
     Reports, 24: 10-21, 1968.

236. Cisin, Ira H. and Cahalan, Don. Some Correlates of American
      Drinking Practices. In: Recent Advances in Studies of Al-
      coholism: An Interdisciplinary Symposium. Ed. Nancy K. Mel-
      lo and Jack H. Mendelson. Publication No. (HSM) 71-9045.
      Washington, D.C.: U.S. Government Printing Office, 1971,
      pages 805-824.

237. Clark, C.D. A Comparison of the Driving Records and Other Charac-
      teristics of Three Alcohol-Involved Populations and a Random
      Sample of Drivers. HIT, 2(10): 1-5, 1972.

238. Clark, Walter. Demographic Characteristics of Tavern Patrons in
      San Francisco. Quarterly Journal of Studies on Alcohol,
      27(2): 316-327, 1966.

239. Clarke, P.R.F., Wyke, M. and Zangwill, O.L. Language Disorder in
      a Case of Korsakoff's Syndrome. Journal of Neurology and
      Psychiatry, 21: 190-194, 1958.

240. Cleary, P.D. A Standardized Estimator of the Prevalence of Alco-
      holism Based on Mortality Data. Journal of Studies on Alco-
      holism, 40: 408-418, 1979.

241. Clerc, P.D., Manigand, G. and Deparis, M. Œdeme soudain des
      bourses apres ponction d'ascite. [Sudden Scrotal Edema
      Following Paracentesis.] Nouvelle Presse Médicale, 5: 1996,
      1976.

242. Cochrane, A.L., St. Leger, A.S. and Moore, F. Health Service
      "Input" and Mortality "Output" in Developed Countries.
      Journal of Epidemiology and Community Health, 32: 200-205,
      1978.

243. Coffman, J.D. Alcohol Ingestion and Leg Cramps. (Questions and
      Answers.) Journal of the American Medical Association, 240:
      2196, 1978.

244. Cohen, Carl I. and Briggs, Frances. A Storefront Clinic on the
      Bowery. Journal of Studies on Alcohol, 37(9): 1336-1340,
      1976.

245. Cohen, Sidney. Drug Abuse in the Aging Patient. Lex et Scientia,
      11: 217-221, 1975.

246. Cohen, Sidney. Drug Abuse in the Aging Patient. Journal of
      Studies on Alcohol, 37(10): 1455, 1976.

247. Cohen, Sidney. Geriatric Drug Abuse. Drug Abuse and Alcohol
      Newsletter (Vista Hill Foundation), 4(2): 1-4, 1975.

248. Collins, Allan C., Yeager, Toni N., Lebsack, M.E. and Panter,
      S. Scott. Variations in Alcohol Metabolism: Influence of
      Sex and Age. Pharmacology, Biochemistry, and Behavior,
      3(6): 973-978, 1975.

249. Collins, P.B. and Johnson, A.H.   Serum Gamma-Glutamyltransferase
     Activity in Alcoholism. Irish Journal of Medical Science,
     147: 182-186, 1978.

250. Conrad, K. Zur Psychopathologie des amnestischen Symptomen-
     komplexes; Gestaltanalyse einer Korsakowschen Psychose.
     [Contribution to the Psychopathology of the Amnestic Syn-
     drome; Gestalt Analysis of a Case of Korsakoff's Psychosis.]
     Deutsche Zeitschrift für Nervenheilkunde, 170: 35-60, 1953.

251. Cooperberg, P.L., Cohen, M.M. and Graham, M. Ultrasonographically
     Guided Percutaneous Pancreatography: Report of Two Cases.
     American Journal of Roentgenology, 132: 662-663, 1979.

252. Coppin, Victor Eustace H. Life Styles and Social Services on
     Skid Row: A Study of Aging Homeless Men. Doctor of Social
     Work Dissertation, University of Southern California, June
     1974 (University Microfilms No. 74-28,430).

253. Corrigan, Eileen M. Problem Drinkers Seeking Treatment. Mono-
     graph No. 8. New Brunswick, New Jersey: Publications
     Division, Rutgers Center of Alcohol Studies, 1974, especially
     pages 14-15.

254. Cosman, B. Fire Hazard of Florida Water; Pyrogenic Potential in
     Hispanic Folk Medicine. New York State Journal of Medicine,
     78: 1475-1477, 1978.

255. Cosper, Ronald and Mozersky, Kenneth. Social Correlates of
     Drinking and Driving. Quarterly Journal of Studies on Alco-
     hol (Supplement No. 4): 58-117, 1968.

256. Costello, Raymond M., Parsons-Manders, Pamela and Schneider, San-
     dra Lee. Alcoholic Mortality: A 12-Year Follow-up. Amer-
     ican Journal of Drug and Alcohol Abuse, 5(2): 199-210, 1978.

257. Costello, Raymond M. and Schneider, Sandra Lee. Mortality in an
     Alcoholic Cohort. International Journal of the Addictions,
     9(3): 355-363, 1974.

258. Council on Pharmacy and Chemistry. Disulfiram. Journal of the
     American Medical Association, 151: 1408-1409, 1953.

259. Courrier, A., Dury, P. and Arbogast, J. Utilisation du tiapride
     en médecine interne. [Use of Tiapride in Internal Medicine.]
     Semaine des Hôpitaux de Paris, 54(21-24): 733-737, 1978.

260. Cowdry, E.V. Aging Better. Springfield, Illinois: C.C. Thomas,
     1972.

261. Craik, Fergus I.M. Similarities between the Effects of Aging and
     Alcoholic Intoxication on Memory Performance, Construed with-
     in a "Levels of Processing" Framework. In: Alcohol and
     Human Memory. Ed. Isabel M. Birnbaum and Elizabeth S. Parker.
     Hilldale, New Jersey: Lawrence Erlbaum Associates, 1977,
     pages 9-21.

262. Cramer, Mary Jane and Blacker, Edward. "Early" and "Late" Problem
     Drinkers among Female Prisoners. Journal of Health and Human
     Behavior, 4: 282-290, 1963.

263. Creutzfeldt, W. and Beck, K. Erhebungen über Ätiologie, Patho-
     genese, Therapieerfolge und Überlebenszeit an einem unaus-
     gewählten Krankengut von 560 Patienten mit Leberzirrhose.
     [Considerations on Etiology, Pathogenesis, Therapeutic Suc-
     cesses, and Survival Time in an Unselected Sample of 560
     Patients with Liver Cirrhosis.] Deutsche Medizinische Wochen-
     schrift, 91: 682-689, 1966.

264. Crispino, L. and Meloni, S. Contributo allo studio sull'alcoolis-
     mo e sulle psicosi alcooliche nei degenti presso l'Ospedale
     Psichiatrico Provinciale di Bergamo nel trentennio 1940-1969.
     [Contribution to the Study of Alcoholism and the Alcoholic
     Psychoses among Inpatients at the Provincial Psychiatric Hos-
     pital of Bergamo during the Three Decades of 1940-1969.]
     Difesa Sociale, 50: 17-44, 1971.

265. Cuervo Muñoz, C. Hipopotasemia en el alcoholismo. [Hypopotas-
     semia in Alcoholism.] Medicina Espanola, 42: 341-344, 1959.

266. Cullen, K.J. and Woodings, T. Alcohol, Tobacco and Analgesics--
     Busselton, 1972. Medical Journal of Australia, 62: 211-214,
     1975.

267. Cushman, P., Jr. Abstinence Following Detoxification and Metha-
     done Maintenance Treatment. American Journal of Medicine,
     65(1): 46-52, 1978.

268. Cushnie, J.M., Ben-Tovim, D.I. and Kopelman, P. Chlormethiazole
     Addiction: Unusual Presentation. British Medical Journal,
     2: 355, 1978.

269. Cutshall, Benjamin J. The Saunders-Sutton Syndrome: An Analysis
     of Delirium Tremens. Quarterly Journal of Studies on Alco-
     hol, 26(3): 423-448, 1965.

270. Cutting, John. Patterns of Performance in Amnesic Subjects.
     Journal of Neurology, Neurosurgery, and Psychiatry, 41: 278-
     282, 1978.

271. Cutting, John. Specific Psychological Deficits in Alcoholism.
     British Journal of Psychiatry, 133: 119-122, 1978.

272. Cutting, John. The Relationship between Korsakov's Syndrome and
     "Alcoholic Dementia." British Journal of Psychiatry, 132:
     240-251, 1978.

273. Czeizel, E. Az alkoholista nők terhességének epidemiológiai
     vizsgalata. [Epidemiological Study on the Pregnancy of
     Women Alcoholics.] Alkohológia, 9: 12-16, 1978.

D

274. Dahl, S. Erfahrungen mit chronischen Alkoholikern in Schweden und Dänemark. [Experiences with Chronic Alcoholics in Sweden and Denmark.] Psychiatrie, Neurolologie und Medizinische Psychologie, 19: 361-366, 1967.

275. Dahl, S. Morbus Alcoholicus. [Alcoholic Morbidity.] Deutsches Medizinisches Journal, 19: 73-76, 1968.

276. Dahlberg, G. Dödlighet bland alkoholister. [Mortality among Alcoholics.] Svenska Läkartidningen, 49: 112-118, 1952.

277. Dahlberg, Gunnar. Suicide, Alcohol, and War. Acta Genetica et Statistica Medica, 1: 191-198, 1948-1949.

278. Dahlgren, K.G. On Death-Rates and Causes of Death in Alcohol Addicts. Acta Psychiatrica et Neurologica Scandinavica, 26(3-4): 297-311, 1951.

279. Dahlgren, L. Female Alcoholics. IV. Marital Situation and Husbands. Acta Psychiatrica Scandinavica, 59(1): 59-69, 1979.

280. Dajer, Fernando, Guevara, Luis, Arosamena, Leopoldo, Suárez, Gloria Irene and Kershenobich, David. Consideraciones sobre la epidemiologia de la cirrosis hepatica alcoholica en Mexico. [Epidemiological Aspects of Alcoholic Liver Cirrhosis in Mexico.] Reviesta de Investigacion Clinica, 30(1): 13-28, 1978.

281. Damrau, Frederic and Liddy, Emma. The Use of Vodka in Geriatrics. Industrial Medicine and Surgery, 31: 463-464, 1962.

282. Damrau, Frederic, Liddy, Emma and Damrau, Adeline Maneery. Value of Stout as a Sedative and Relaxing Soporific. Journal of the American Geriatrics Society, 11: 238-241, 1963.

283. Daniel, R. Five-Year Study of 693 Psychogeriatric Admissions in Queensland. Geriatrics, 27: 132-155, 1972.

284. Daniel, R. Psychiatric Drug Use and Abuse in the Aged. Geri-
      atrics, 25: 144-145, 148-151, 154-155, 158, 1970.

285. Davis, Harry L., White, William G. and Sutliff, Wheelan D. Char-
      acteristics of Hospitalized Tuberculous Patients Today.
      Southern Medical Journal, 71(11): 1401-1403, 1978.

286. Davis, J.H., Hirschman, J.H., Nagel, E.L. and Nussenfeld, R.D.
      Alcohol Benefit for the Geriatric Patient. Journal of the
      American Medical Association, 227(4): 439-440, 1974.

287. Davis, R.E. and Smith, B.K. Pyridoxal and Folate Deficiency in
      Alcoholics. Medical Journal of Australia, 2(10): 357-360,
      1974.

288. Day, Nancy. Estimates of the Role of Alcohol in Mortality.
      Drinking and Drug Practice Surveyor, 11: 18-23, 1976.

289. De Brito-Paiva, E. Aspectos somáticos del alcoholismo en la
      practica geriátrica. [Somatic Aspects of Alcoholism in
      Geriatric Practice.] Revista Espagñola de Gerontologia, 13:
      75-78, 1978.

290. Decker, J.B., Wells, C.E. and McDowell, F. Cerebellar Dysfunction
      Associated with Chronic Alcoholism. Neurology, 9: 361-366,
      1959.

291. Decker, K. Hirndurchblutung nach Biergenuss. [Cerebral Circu-
      lation after Drinking Beer.] Münchener Medizinische Wochen-
      schrift, 117: 567-570, 1975.

292. De Faire, U., Friberg, L., Lorich, U. and Lundman, T. A Valida-
      tion of Cause-of-Death Certification in 1,156 Deaths. Acta
      Medica Scandinavica, 200(3): 223-228, 1976.

293. Delay, J., Boudin, G., Brion, S. and Barbizet, J. Etude anatomo-
      clinique de huit encéphalopathies alcooliques: Encéphalo-
      pathie de Gayet-Wernicke et syndromes voisins. [Anatomical
      and Clinical Study of Eight Cases of Alcoholic Encephal-
      opathy: Gayet-Wernicke's Encephalopathy and Related Syn-
      dromes.] Revue Neurologique, 94: 596-601, 1956.

294. Del Fabbro, Valentino and Greco, Sergio. L'opera del medico sana-
      toriale nell'associazione alcoolismo cronico e tubercolosi.
      [Performance of Sanatorium Physicians in the Association of
      Chronic Alcoholism and Tuberculosis.] Minerva Medica, 54:
      539-542, 1963.

295. DeMoura, M. Carneiro, Correia, J. Pinto and Madeira, F. Clinical
      Alcohol Hypoglycemia. Annals of Internal Medicine, 66(5):
      893-905, 1967.

296. De Nicholas, P. Rapporti tra alcool e meccanismi dell'emostasi
      nell'anziano. [Report on Alcohol and the Mechanisms of
      Hemostasis in the Elderly.] Giornale di Gerontologia, 15(1):
      27, 1967.

297. DeParis, M., Leluc, R., Manigand, G., Auzépy, P. and Delluc, G.
      Le coma hypoglycémique provoqué par absorption d'alcool chez
      l'adulte; remarques cliniques et pathogéniques à propos d'une
      observation. [Hypoglycemic Coma Caused by Absorption of Al-
      cohol in the Adult; Clinical and Pathological Remarks with
      Reference to One Case.] Revue de l'Alcoolisme, 12: 104-117,
      1966. (This article also appears as: L'hypoglycémie al-
      coolique; à propos d'une observation chez un malade atteint
      d'un syndrome carentiel post-gastrectomie. [Alcoholic Hypo-
      glycemia; Observation in a Patient with a Postgastrectomy
      Deficiency Syndrome.] Semaine des Hôpitaux de Paris, 43:
      858-867, 1967.)

298. DéRobert, L. Evolution de l'alcoolisme en France en 1943.
      [The Evolution of Alcoholism in France in 1943.] Recreil
      der Travau de la Institut Nationale d'Hygiene, 2(1): 113-122,
      1945.

299. DéRobert, L. Evolution de l'alcoolisme en France en 1946. [Evo-
      lution of Alcoholism in France in 1946.] Bulletin de l'In-
      stitut National d'Hygiene, 3: 6-11, 1948.

300. DéRobert, L. Evolution de l'alcoolisme en France en 1947.
      [Evolution of Alcoholism in France in 1947.] Bulletin de
      l'Institut National d'Hygiene, 3: 578-584, 1948.

301. Deruty, R., Dechaume, J.-P., Lecuire, J., Bret, P. and El Ouar-
      zazi, A. Traitement microchirurgical d'une série d'anévrysmes
      arteriels intra-crâniens sus-tentoriels. [Microsurgical
      Treatment of a Series of Arterial Intracranial Supratenorial
      Aneurysms.] Neuro-Chirurgie, 22(3): 227-238, 1976.

302. Descos, L., M'Bendi, S., Sassolas, G., Audigier, J.-C., Sid-
      iqian, N., Faure, A. and Bizollon, C.-A. Dosage de l'insu-
      line et de l'hormone de croissance plasmatiques au cours de
      l'épreuve d'hyperglycémie provoquée par voie orale dans la
      cirrhose alcoolique. [Measurement of Plasma Insulin and
      Growth Hormone during the Oral Glucose Tolerance Test in
      Patients with Alcoholic Cirrhosis.] Archives Françaises des
      Maladies de l'Appareil Digestif, 63: 17-24, 1974.

303. Dessemond-Negroni, M., Pauli, A.M., Charbit, J.J., Gauthier, C.
      and François, G. Carence en thiamine chez les éthyliques
      chroniques; intérêt du traitement pré et post opératoire.
      [Thiamine deficiency in chronic alcoholics; Value of Pre-
      and Postoperative Treatment.] Annales del'Anesthesiologie
      Française, 18: 853-856, 1977.

304. Di Blasi, G. and Gaglio, L. L'incidenza delle psicotossicosi al-
      cooliche nella provincia di Torino; rilievi statistici e con-
      siderazioni medico-legali. [Incidence of Alcoholic Psychoses
      in the Province of Torino; a Statistical Review and Medico-
      legal Considerations.] Difesa Sociale, 48: 229-242, 1969.

305. Dietrich, Heinz and Herle, Luise. Über Alter, Socialschicht,
     Mobilität und Wohnort chronischer Alkoholiker. [On Age,
     Social Stratum, Mobility, and Place of Residence of Chronic
     Alcoholics.] Kölner Zeitschrift für Soziologie und Sozial-
     psychologie, 15: 277-294, 1963.

306. Dion, C., Simard, N., Carle, R. and Roberge, M.-L. Étude com-
     parative du chlodiazepoxide et du MgSO$_4$ hypertonique dans le
     syndrome de sevrage à l'alcool. [Comparative Study of Chlor-
     diazepoxide and Hypertonic MgSO$_4$ in the Alcohol Withdrawal
     Syndrome.] Revue de l'Alcoolisme, 14: 132-148, 1968. (Also
     in: Laval Médicale, 39: 222-231, 1968.)

307. Dipsomania in the Aged. (Any Questions?) British Medical Jour-
     nal, 1: 832, 1951.

308. Ditman, K.S. and Benor, D. Diazepam (Valium) Very High Dose:
     Longitudinal and Single Case Study. Western Medicine, 5:
     109-110, 1966.

309. Divisia, A. and Girard-Madoux, M. Une nouvelle approche thera-
     peutique en neurologie. [A New Therapeutical Approach in
     Neurology.] Semaine des Hôpitaux de Paris, 54(41-42): 1265-
     1268, 1978.

310. Dobbie, Judy. One for the End of the Road: Alcoholism and Drug
     Abuse among the Elderly. Macleans, 90: 66-67, 1977.

311. Dobbie, Judy. Sour Notes from the Vintage Years: Substance
     Abuse among the Elderly. Addictions, 24(3): 58-75, 1977.
     (Reprinted as: Substance Abuse among the Elderly. Toronto:
     Addiction Research Foundation of Ontario, 1978, pages 1-17.)

312. Dobrzański, T. Growth Hormone (HGH), IRI and Total IRI Responses
     to Glucose Load in Selected Groups of Mental Patients.
     III. Studies in Insulin-Treated Diabetics under Phenothiazine
     Treatment or with Delirium Tremens. Endokrynologia Polska,
     25: 461-466, 1974.

313. Docter, Richard F. Drinking Practices of Skid Row Alcoholics.
     Quarterly Journal of Studies on Alcohol, 28(4): 700-708,
     1967.

314. D'Orban, P.T. Habitual Drunkenness Offenders in Holloway Pris-
     on. In: Proceedings of an International Symposium on
     The Drunkenness Offense held from 15 to 17 May, 1968, at the
     Institute of Psychiatry, Maudsley Hospital, London, S.E.5.
     under the Auspices of Camberwell Council on Alcoholism and
     International Council on Alcohol and Addictions. Ed. Tim-
     othy Cook, Dennis Gath, and Celia Hensman. Oxford: Perga-
     mon Press, 1969, pages 51-62, especially pages 54-59.

315. Dournovo, P., Garaix, J.-P., Corcelle, P., Poirson, B. and Ay-
      ral, X. Aspergillose broncho-pulmonaire aiguë non septi-
      cémique: observation chez un malade sans déficit immuni-
      taire patent. [Acute Nonsepticemic Bronchopulmonary Asper-
      gillosis: One Case in a Patient with No Obvious Immune
      Deficiency.] Nouvelle Presse Médicale, 7: 1093-1095, 1978.

316. Drew, Leslie R.H. Alcohol. Medical Journal of Australia, 66:
      238, 1979.

317. Drew, Leslie R.H. Alcoholism as a Self-Limiting Disease. Quar-
      terly Journal of Studies on Alcohol, 29: 956-967, 1968.

318. Dreyfus, A. Kasuistischer Beitrag zur Frage der chronischen
      Methylalkoholvergiftung. [Contribution to the Problem of
      Chronic Methyl Alcohol Poisoning; Case Report.] Zeitschrift
      für Unfallmedizin und Berufskrankheiten, 39: 84-90, 1946.

319. Droller, Hugo. Some Aspects of Alcoholism in the Elderly.
      The Lancet, 2: 137-139, 1964.

320. Drug Use among the Elderly. Stash Capsules, 7(3): 1-6, 1975.

321. Duckworth, Grace L. and Rosenblatt, Adylin. Helping the Elderly
      Alcoholic. Social Casework, 57(5): 296-301, 1976.

322. Duncalf, D. and Kipes, E.R. Geriatric Anesthesia. In: Clinical
      Geriatrics. Ed. I. Rossman. Philadelphia: J.B. Lippincott,
      1971, pages 421-437.

323. Duncan, D. and Vogel-Sprott, M. Drinking Habits of Impaired
      Drivers. Blutalkohol, 15: 252-260, 1978.

324. Dunlop, T.W. The Alcadd Test: An Extension of Norms. American
      Journal of Drug and Alcohol Abuse, 5(2): 211-220, 1978.

325. Dunn, G.R., Wilson, Thomas G. and Jacobson, K. Bruce. Age-Depen-
      dent Changes in Alcohol Dehydrogenase in Drosophilia. Jour-
      nal of Experimental Zoology, 171: 185-189, 1969.

326. Durand, Douglas E. Effects of Drinking on the Power and Affili-
      ation Needs of Middle-Aged Females. Journal of Clinical
      Psychology, 31(3): 549-553, 1975.

E

327. Eakins, W.A. and Faloon, D. The Profile of the Suspect Drunk-in-Charge Driver in the Belfast Area. Ulster Medical Journal, 46: 32-37, 1977.

328. Ebels, E.J. How Common Is Wernicke-Korsakoff Syndrome? The Lancet, 2: 781-782, 1978.

329. Eckardt, Michael J. Consequences of Alcohol and Other Drug Use in the Aged. In: The Biology of Aging. Ed. John A. Behnke, Caleb E. Finch, and Gairdner B. Moment. New York: Plenum Publishing Corporation, 1978.

330. Economacos, G. Neurological Complications of Spinal Analgesia. [Letter.] Anaesthesia, 33(4): 374, 1978.

331. Edwards, Griffith, Chandler, Jane and Hensman, Celia. Drinking in a London Suburb. I. Correlates of Normal Drinking. Quarterly Journal of Studies on Alcohol (Supplement No. 6): 69-93, 1972.

332. Edwards, Griffith, Chandler, Jane, Hensman, Celia and Peto, Julian. Drinking in a London Suburb. II. Correlates of Trouble with Drinking among Men. Quarterly Journal of Studies on Alcohol (Supplement No. 6): 94-1972.

333. Edwards, Griffith, Hawker, Ann, Hensman, Celia, Peto, Julian and Williamson, Valerie. Alcoholics Known or Unknown to Agencies: Epidemiological Studies in a London Suburb. British Journal of Psychiatry, 123: 169-183, 1973.

334. Edwards, Griffith, Kyle, Elspeth and Nicholls, Peter. Alcoholics Admitted to Four Hospitals in England. I. Social Class and the Interaction of Alcoholics with the Treatment System. Quarterly Journal of Studies on Alcohol, 35(2): 499-522, 1974.

335. Edwards, Griffith, Kyle, Elspeth, Nicholls, Peter and Taylor, C. Alcoholism and Correlates of Mortality: Implications for Epidemiology. Journal of Studies on Alcohol, 39(9): 1607-1617, 1978.

336. Effects of Retirement on Drinking Behavior. National Council on the Aging, Research and Evaluation Department, Washington, D.C., 1977.

337. Ehrsam, John L. Issues Involving Aging and the Aged. Paper presented at Conference on Aging, 19-20 April, 1977, Hershey, Pennsylvania.

338. Elder, Thomas C. Alcoholism and its Onset in a Population of Admitted Alcoholics (An AA Study). British Journal of Addiction, 68: 291-294, 1973.

339. Elderly Drinking Patterns Are Studied. Alcoholism Newsletter, 1(3): 1, 1979.

340. Elderly Program Development Center, Inc. Alcoholism and the Elderly: A Study of Problems and Prospects. Iowa City, Iowa: Elderly Program Development Center, 1976.

341. Elias, Merrill F. Cognition Revisited: Aging as Viewed by a Laboratory Psychologist. Contemporary Psychology, 24(5): 418-419, 1979.

342. Elmfeldt, Dag, Wilhelmsson, Claes, Vedin, Anders, Tibblin, Gösta and Wilhelmsen, Lars. Characteristics of Representative Male Survivors of Myocardial Infarction Compared with Representative Population Samples. Acta Medica Scandinavica, 199: 387-398, 1976.

343. Encel, S. and Kotowicz, K. Heavy Drinking and Alcoholism; Preliminary Report. Medical Journal of Australia, 1: 607-612, 1970.

344. Encel, S., Kotowicz, K.C. and Resler, H.E. Drinking Patterns in Sydney, Australia. Quarterly Journal of Studies on Alcohol (Supplement No. 6): 1-27, 1972.

345. Entin, G.M. Klinika i terapiya alkogol'nykh psikhozov v pozhilom voraste. [The Clinical Picture and Treatment of Alcoholic Psychoses in Old Age.] Zhurnal Nevropatologii i Psikhiatrii Imeni S.S. Korsakova, 70: 743-750, 1970.

346. Epstein, Leon J., Mills, C. and Simon, Alexander. Antisocial Behavior and the Elderly. Comprehensive Psychiatry, 11(1): 36-42, 1970.

347. Epstein, Leon J., Mills, C. and Simon, Alexander. Antisocial Behavior of the Elderly. California Mental Health Research Digest, 8(2): 78-79, 1970.

348. Epstein, Leon J., Mills, C. and Simon, Alexander. The Elderly
      Offender. I. The Elderly Alcoholic: The Jail as a Substi-
      tute for Hospitalization. Paper Presented at the Annual
      Meeting of the Gerontological Society, Denver, Colorado,
      1968.

349. Epstein, Leon J. and Simon, Alexander. Organic Brain Syndrome in
      the Elderly. Geriatrics, 22(2): 145-150, 1967.

350. Epstein, P.S., Pisani, V.D. and Fawcett, J.A. Alcoholism and
      Cerebral Atrophy. Alcoholism, 1(1): 61-65, 1977.

351. Eriksen, B.O. and Kløvrud, P. Sosial bakgrunn for alkoholikere i
      Blåkorsklinikken, Oslo 1969; utdrag av undersøkelse foretatt
      i forbindelse med hovedoppgave ved Norges Kommunal- og Sosial-
      skole. [Social Background of Alcoholics in the Blåkors
      Clinic, Oslo 1969; Extract from a Study Done in Connection
      with the Main Work of the Norwegian Communal and Social
      School.] Tidsskrift for den Norske Laegeforening, 91: 190-
      193, 1971.

352. Ernst, A. John, Dempster, John P., Yee, Randall, St. Dennis,
      Clarke and Nakano, Loren. Alcohol Toxicity, Blood Alcohol
      Concentration and Body Water in Young and Adult Rats. Jour-
      nal of Studies on Alcohol, 37(3): 347-356, 1976.

353. Ernst, J. and Choteau, P. Une approche des manifestations psy-
      chiatriques de l'éthylisme. [An Approach to the Psychiatric
      Manifestations of Alcoholism.] Semaine des Hôpitaux de
      Paris, 54(17-20): 649-652, 1978.

354. Experimental Aging Research. Biochemical and Behavioral Review,
      2(6): 543-562, 1976.

F

355. Fact Sheet: Alcohol and the Elderly. Rockville, Maryland: National Institute on Alcohol Abuse and Alcoholism and National Clearinghouse for Alcohol Information, 1977.

356. Faden, Vivian B. Primary Diagnosis of Discharges from Non-Federal General Hospital Psychiatric Inpatient Units, United States. Mental Health Statistical Note, 137: 1-23, especially pages 19-22, 1977.

357. Falconer, M.W., Altamura, M.V. and Behnke, H.D. Aging Patients: A Guide for Their Care. New York: Springer Publishing Co., 1976.

358. Falkey, D. Bruce and Schneyer, Solomon. Characteristics of Male Alcoholics Admitted to the Medical Ward of a General Hospital. Quarterly Journal of Studies on Alcohol, 18(1): 67-97, 1957.

359. Fann, William E. Pharmacotherapy in Older Depressed Patients. Journal of Gerontology, 31(3): 304-310, 1976.

360. Favre, A. and de Meuron, B. Aspect psychosocial de l'alcoolisme du 3e âge. [Psychosocial Aspects of Alcoholism in Old Age.] Praxis, 52(22): 711-716, 1963.

361. Fedotov, D.D. and Chudin, A.S. O suitsidal'nykh popytkakh v involyutsionnom i starcheskom periodakh. [Suicide Attempts during the Periods of Involution and Senility.] Zhurnal Nevropatologii i Psikhiatrii Imeni S.S. Korsakova, 76: 406-409, 1976.

362. Fedrizzi, G. Alcoolismo ed apparato oculare nella vecchiaia. [Alcoholism and Ocular Apparatus in Old Age.] Giornale di Gerontologia, 15: 75-83, 1967.

363. Feinfeld, D.A. and Carvounis, C.P. Fatal Hyperkalemia and Hyperchloremic Acidosis: Association with Spironolactone in the Absence of Renal Impairment. Journal of the American Medical Association, 240: 1516, 1978.

364. Feldman, Joseph, Su, Wen Huey, Kaley, Maureen M. and Kissin, Ben-
       jamin. Skid Row and Inner-City Alcoholics; a Comparison of
       Drinking Patterns and Medical Problems. Quarterly Journal
       of Studies on Alcohol, 35(2): 565-576, 1974.

365. Fernandez, David. Another Esophageal Rupture after Alcohol and
       Disulfiram. New England Journal of Medicine, 286: 610, 1972.

366. Ferrario, Elizabeth A. Community Nursing Care Study: Seeking
       Oblivion. Nursing Times, 73: 527, 1977.

367. Feuerlein, W. Klinisch-statistische Untersuchungen über die
       Entstehungsbedingungen und die Prognose des Alkoholdelirs.
       [Clinical Statistical Studies on the Etiological Conditions
       and the Prognosis of Alcoholic Delirium.] Der Nervenarzt,
       38: 206-212, 1967.

368. Feuerlein, W. and Heyse, H. Echoencephalographische Messungen
       der Weite des 3. Ventrikels bei Alkoholikern. [Echoenceph-
       alographic Measurements of the Width of the 3d Ventricle in
       Alcoholics.] Alcoholism, 5: 85-89, 1969. (Also as: Die
       Weite der 3. Hirnkammer bei Alkoholikern; Ergebnisse echo-
       enzephalographischer Messungen. [Width of the 3d Ventricle
       in Alcoholics; Results of Echoencephalographic Measurements.]
       Archiv für Psychiatrie und Nervenkrankheiten, 213: 78-85,
       1970.)

369. Feuerlein, W. and Kunstmann, G. Die Häufigkeit des Alkoholismus;
       Vergleich zwischen verschiedenen Krankenanstalten. [The In-
       cidence of Alcoholism; Comparison between Various Hospitals.]
       Münchener Medizinischer Wochenschrift, 115: 1991-1996, 1973.

370. Fialkov, M.J. Alcoholics and the Emergency Ward. Part I. Clin-
       ical Characteristics. South African Medical Journal, 52:
       613-616, 1977.

371. Fine, E.W. and Scoles, P. Secondary Prevention of Alcoholism
       Using a Population of Offenders Arrested for Driving While
       Intoxicated. Annals of the New York Academy of Sciences,
       273: 637-645, 1976.

372. Fitz-Gerald, Frances L., Barfield, M. Ashton and Warrington, R.J.
       Voluntary Alcohol Consumption in Chimpanzees and Orangutans.
       Quarterly Journal of Studies on Alcohol, 29(2): 330-336, 1968.

373. Fitzgerald, G.A. and Balcavage, W.X. Consequences of Dietary
       Ethanol on Permeability and Respiration of Mitochondria and
       Liver ADH in Young and Aged Rats. In: Currents in Alco-
       holism. Volume 5: Biomedical Issues and Clinical Effects of
       Alcoholism. Ed. M. Galanter. New York: Grune and Stratton,
       1979, pages 91-100.

374. Fitzgerald, G.A. and Balcavage, W.X. Dietary Ethanol-Induced
       Changes in Mitochondria from Young and Aged Animals. Alco-
       holism: Clinical and Experimental Research, 2(2): 188, 1978.

375. Fornaro, L. Funzionalità gastrica e crasi ematica nell'ambliopia
      alcoolico-tabagica. [Gastric Function and Blood Crasis in
      Alcohol-Tobacco Amblyopia.] Rivista Oto-Neuro-Oftalmologica,
      31: 44-59, 1956.

376. Forni, Peter J. Alcohol and the Elderly. In: Drugs and the
      Elderly, ed. Ronald C. Kayne. Rev. ed. Los Angeles, Cali-
      fornia: The Ethel Percy Andrus Gerontology Center, Univer-
      sity of Southern California Press, 1978, Chapter 7, pages 75-
      83.

377. Foulds, G.A. and Hassall, Christine. The Significance of Age of
      Onset of Excessive Drinking in Male Alcoholics. British
      Journal of Psychiatry, 115: 1027-1032, 1969.

378. Fourtanier, G., Bornet, J.-L., Jean-Noël, M., Lacroix, A. and
      Escat, J. Utilisation de la vasopressine au cours des deri-
      vations portales. [Use of Vasopressin during Portal Bypass.]
      Nouvelle Presse Médicale, 8: 503-504, 1979.

379. Fox, J.H., Ramsey, R.G., Huckman, M.S., and Proske, A.E. Cerebral
      Ventricular Enlargement; Chronic Alcoholics Examined by
      Computerized Tomography. Journal of the American Medical
      Association, 236: 365-368, 1976.

380. Fox, V. Intelligence, Race, and Age as Selective Factors in
      Crime. Journal of Criminal Law and Criminology, 37: 141-152,
      1946.

381. Frank, H., Heil, W. and Leodolter, I. Leber und Bierkonsum;
      vergleichende Untersuchungen an 450 Arbeitern. [Beer Con-
      sumption and the Liver; Comparative Studies in 450 Workers.]
      Münchener Medizinischer Wochenschrift, 109: 892-897, 1967.

382. Frank, O. Nutritional State and Purine Metabolism. Advances in
      Experimental Medicine and Biology, 76B: 266-268, 1977.

383. Frayssinet, R., Sahel, J. and Sarles, H. Les wirsungorragies;
      étude d'un cas et revue de la littérature. [Hemorrhage of
      the Pancreatic Duct; Report of a Case and Review of the
      Literature.] Gastroentérologie Clinique et Biologique, 2:
      993-1000, 1978.

384. Freeman, Joseph T. Some Common Cardiovascular Agents. In: Clin-
      ical Principles and Drugs in the Aging. Ed. Joseph T. Free-
      man. Springfield, Illinois: Charles C. Thomas, 1963,
      pages 383-404.

385. Freese, A.S. The End of Senility. New York: Arbor House, 1978.

386. Fresneau, M. L'alcoolisme des vieillards à Angers. [Alcoholism
      in the Elderly in Angers.] Revue de l'Alcoolisme, 15: 58-60,
      1969.

387. Freund, G. Possible Relationships of Alcohol in Membranes to
      Cancer. Cancer Research, 39: 2899-2901, 1979.

388. Freund, Gerhard. The Effect of Ethanol and Aging on the Trans-
      port of $\propto$-Aminoisobutyric Acid into the Brain. Brain Re-
      search, 46: 363-368, 1972.

389. Freund, Gerhard. The Effects of Chronic Alcohol and Vitamin E
      Consumption on Aging Pigments and Learning Performance in
      Mice. Life Sciences, 24(2): 145-151, 1979.

390. Freyhan, F.A. Conversion Hysteria in an Individual Suffering
      from a Korsakoff Psychosis. Delaware State Medical Journal,
      16: 95-98, 1944.

391. Friedman, G.D., Dales, L.G. and Ury, H.K. Mortality in Middle-
      Aged Smokers and Nonsmokers. New England Journal of Medi-
      cine, 300: 213-217, 1979.

392. Funk, Louis P. and Prescott, John H. Study Shows Wine Aids
      Patient Attitudes. Modern Hospital, 108: 182-184, 1967.

393. Funkhouser, Marilyn Joy. Identifying Alcohol Problems among
      Elderly Hospital Patients. Alcohol Health and Research
      World, 2(2): 27-34, 1977-78.

G

394. Gabelic, I. Geriatric Service and Geriatric Club. Anali Bolnice Dr. M. Stojanovic, 10(2): 221-226, 1971.

395. Gaeta, Michael J. and Gaetano, Ronald J. The Elderly: Their Health and the Drugs in Their Lives. Dubuque, Iowa: Kendall-Hunt Publishers, 1977.

396. Gaetano, Ronald J. and Epstein, B. Drugs and the Elderly. In: First International Action Conference on Substance Abuse, November 9-13, 1977. Volume 3. Intervention and Prevention. Phoenix, Arizona: Do It Now Foundation, 1979, pages 123-140.

397. Gaetano, Ronald J. and Gaeta, Michael J. Strategies for Dealing with Substance Abuse among the Elderly, pages 270-279. [See Entry #1114.]

398. Gaillard, André and Perrin, Paul. L'alcoolisme des personnes âgées. [Alcoholism in Aged Persons.] Revue de l'Alcoolisme, 15: 5-32, 1969.

399. Gaitz, Charles M. and Baer, Paul E. Characteristics of Elderly Patients with Alcoholism. Archives of General Psychiatry, 24(4): 372-378, 1971.

400. Galdi, Z. and Vertes, L. A "gero-alkohológia" néhány aktuális kérdéséről. [On Some Topical Questions of Gerontological Alcohology.] Alkohológia, 8: 17-18, 1977.

401. Gall, M. von and Becker, H. Zur Anwendung der Computertomographie (CT) in der klinischen Psychiatrie. [On the Use of Computer Tomography (CT) in Clinical Psychiatry.] Fortschritte der Neurologie Psychiatrie und ihrer Grenzgebiete, 46: 361-368, 1978.

402. Galvão-Teles, A., Anderson, D.C., Burke, C.W., Marshall, J.C., Corker, C.S., Bown, R.L. and Clark, M.L. Biologically Active Androgens and Oestradiol in Men with Chronic Liver Disease. The Lancet, 1: 173-177, 1973.

403. Garb, J.L., Brown, R.B., Garb, J.R. and Tuthill, R.W. Differences
      in Etiology of Pneumonias in Nursing Home and Community
      Patients. Journal of the American Medical Association, 240:
      2169-2172, 1978.

404. Garetz, Floyd K. Common Psychiatric Syndromes of the Aged. Min-
      nesota Medicine, 57: 618-620, 1974.

405. Garrett, Gerald R. and Bahr, Howard M. Women on Skid Row. Quar-
      terly Journal of Studies on Alcohol, 34(4): 1228-1243, 1973.

406. Garros, B. and Bouvier, M.H. Excès de la surmortalité masculine
      en France et causes médicales de décès. [Excessive Mortality
      among Men in France and the Medical Causes of Death.] Popu-
      lation, 33: 1095-1114, 1978.

407. Gath, Dennis. The Male Drunk in Court. In: Proceedings of an
      International Symposium on The Drunkenness Offence held
      15 to 17 May, 1968, at the Institute of Psychiatry, Mauds-
      ley Hospital, London, S.E.5. under the Auspices of Camber-
      well Council on Alcoholism and International Council on
      Alcohol and Addictions. Ed. Timothy Cook, Dennis Gath, and
      Celia Hensman. Oxford: Pergamon Press, 1969, pages 9-26,
      especially pages 13-14.

408. Geest, H. The Psychological Aspects of the Aging Process with
      Sociological Implications. St. Louis: Warren H. Green,
      1968.

409. Gelli, B.R. Considerazioni sulla psicogenesis e sociogenesi
      dell'alcoolismo femminile nel Salento; in base a rilievi
      clinico-statistici su alcooliste ricoverate nel ventennio
      1945-1964. [Considerations on the Psychogenesis and Socio-
      genesis of Female Alcoholism in Salento; Based on Clinical-
      Statistical Findings in Alcoholics Hospitalized in the 20-
      Year Period 1945-1964.] Ospedale Psichiatrico, 33: 539-582,
      1965.

410. Gerber, J.A. The Chronic Alcoholic in a Small Community Hospital.
      Maryland State Medical Journal, 23(9): 79-80, 1974.

411. Geriatric Alcoholism and Drug Abuse. Gerontologist, 17(2): 168-
      174, 1977.

412. Gerke, G. Intravenöse Reinfusionsbehandlung bei therapierefrak-
      tärem Aszites. [Intravenous Reinfusion in Patients with
      Treatment-Resistant Ascites.] Deutsche Medizinische Wochen-
      schrift, 104, 95-98, 1979.

413. Gerlach, D. and Von Ohlen, W.D. Alcohol-Induced Cardiomyopathy.
      Beiträge zur Gerichtlichen Medizin, 36: 359-367, 1978.

414. Gertler, Robert. Alcohol Consumption and Coronary-Artery
      Disease. (Letter.) The New England Journal of Medicine,
      297(22): 1234-1235, 1977.

415. Geschwind, N. Organic Problems in the Aged: Brain Syndromes
     and Alcoholism. (Discussion.) Journal of Geriatric Psy-
     chiatry, 11(2): 161-166, 1978.

416. Gibson, John, Johansen, Arne, Rawson, Graeme and Webster, Ian.
     Drinking, Smoking and Drug-Taking Patterns in a Predominantly
     Lower Socioeconomic Status Sample: Comparison with Medicheck
     Sample. Medical Journal of Australia, 2(14): 459-461, 1977.

417. Gilbert, J.G. Understanding Old Age. New York: Ronald Press,
     1952.

418. Giller, E.L., Jr., Bialos, D.S., Docherty, J.P., Jatlow, P. and
     Harkness, L. Chronic Amitriptyline Toxicity. American
     Journal of Psychiatry, 136: 458-459, 1979.

419. Gillis, L.S. The Mortality Rate and Causes of Death of Treated
     Chronic Alcoholics. South Africa Medical Journal, 43:
     230-232, 1969.

420. Gillis, L.S., Lewis, J. and Slabbert, M. Alcoholism among the
     Cape Coloureds. South Africa Medical Journal, 47: 1374-1382,
     1973.

421. Giovanardi, F. and Johannes, K. Alcoolismo nell'età senile (la
     patologia strettamente etilica). [Alcoholism in the Elderly
     Age (the Strictly Alcoholic Pathology).] Giornale di Geron-
     tologia, 15: 129-135, 1967.

422. Giusti, G., Ruggiero, G., Galanti, B., Piccinino, F., Nardiel-
     lo, S., Russo, M., Galante, D. and Aloisio, V. Etiological,
     Clinical, and Laboratory Data of a Series of Chronic Liver
     Diseases from a Southern Italy Area. Acta Hepato-Gastro-
     enterologica, 25(6): 431-437, 1978.

423. Glatt, Max M. Alcoholism and Drug Dependence--Under One Umbrel-
     la? In: World Dialogue on Alcohol and Drug Dependence.
     Ed. Elizabeth D. Whitney. Boston: Beacon Press, 1970,
     pages 311-366, especially pages 349-350.

424. Glatt, Max M. Drinking Habits of English (Middle Class) Alco-
     holics. Acta Psychiatrica Scandinavica, 37: 88-113, 1961.

425. Glatt, Max M. Experiences with Elderly Alcoholics in England.
     Alcoholism, 2(1): 23-26, 1978.

426. Glatt, Max M. and Rosin, A.J. Aspects of Alcoholism in the El-
     derly. The Lancet, 2: 472-473, 1964.

427. Glatt, Max M., Rosin, A.J. and Jauhar, P. Alcoholic Problems in
     the Elderly. Age and Ageing (Supplement): 64-71, 1978.

428. Glenn, N.D. and Zody, R.E. Cohort Analysis with National Survey
     Data. Gerontologist, 10: 233-240, 1970.

429. Glosser, G., Butters, Nelson and Samuels, I. Failures in Infor-
      mation Processing in Patients with Korsakoff's Syndrome.
      Neuropsychologia, 14: 327-334, 1976.

430. Glover, S.C., McPhie, J.L. and Brunt, P.W. Cholestasis in Acute
      Alcoholic Liver Disease. The Lancet, 2(8052-8053): 1305-
      1307, 1977.

431. Gluckman, Stephen J., Dvorak, Vera C. and MacGregor, Rob Roy.
      Host Defenses during Prolonged Alcohol Consumption in a
      Controlled Environment. Archives of Internal Medicine,
      137: 1539-1543, 1977.

432. Goddard, D. and Drieman, P. Positive Treatment Approaches to the
      Elderly Alcoholic. In: First International Action Confer-
      ence on Substance Abuse, November 9-13, 1977. Volume 1:
      Alcohol: Use and Abuse. Phoenix, Arizona: Do It Now Foun-
      dation, 1979, pages 162-170.

433. Goldstein, Gerald. Perceptual and Cognitive Deficit in Alcohol-
      ics. In: Empirical Studies of Alcoholism. Ed. Gerald Gold-
      stein and Charles Neuringer. Cambridge, Massachusetts:
      Ballinger Publishing Co., 1976, Chapter 5, pages 115-151,
      especially pages 140-141.

434. Goldstein, S. and Grant, A. The Psychogeriatric Patient in Hos-
      pital. Canadian Medical Association Journal, 111: 329-332,
      1974.

435. Goodrich, Charles H. Use of Alcohol by Persons 65 Years and
      Over, Upper East Side of Manhattan. Supplemental Medical
      Observations to the Final Report under Contract HSM-43-73-38
      NIA. Springfield, Virginia: NTIS, 1974. [See Entry #553.]

436. Goodrick, Charles L. Alcohol Preference of the Male Sprague-
      Dawley Albino Rat as a Function of Age. Journal of Geron-
      tology, 22: 369-371, 1967.

437. Goodrick, Charles L. Behavioral Characteristics of Young and
      Senescent Inbred Female Mice of the C57BL/6J Strain. Jour-
      nal of Gerontology, 22: 459-464, 1967.

438. Goodrick, Charles L. Behavioral Differences in Young and Aged
      Mice: Strain Differences for Activity Measures, Operant
      Learning, Sensory Discrimination, and Alcohol Preference.
      Experimental Aging Research, 1(2): 191-207, 1975.

439. Goodrick, Charles L. Ethanol Selection by Inbred Mice: Mode of
      Inheritance and the Effect of Age on the Genetic System.
      Journal of Studies on Alcohol, 39(1): 19-38, 1978.

440. Goodwin, Donald W. Blackouts and Alcohol-Induced Memory Dys-
      function. In: Recent Advances in Studies of Alcoholism:
      An Interdisciplinary Symposium. Ed. Nancy K. Mello and
      Jack H. Mendelson. Publication No. (HSM) 71-9045. Wash-
      ington, D.C.: U.S. Government Printing Office, 1971.

441. Gordon, Judith J., Kirchoff, Karen L. and Philipps, Barton K.
     Alcoholism and the Elderly: A Study of Problems and Pros-
     pects. Iowa City, Iowa: Elderly Program Development Center,
     1976.

442. Gorsuch, R.L. The Impact of Drug Treatments on During-Treatment
     Criteria: 1971-1972 DARP Admissions. American Journal of
     Drug and Alcohol Abuse, 2: 73-98, 1975.

443. Gorwitz, Kurt, Bahn, Anita, Warthen, Frances Jean and Cooper,
     Myles. Some Epidemiological Data on Alcoholism in Maryland:
     Based on Admissions to Psychiatric Facilities. Quarterly
     Journal of Studies on Alcohol, 31(2): 423-443, 1970.

444. Gottfreis, C.G., Oreland, L., Wiberg, A. and Winblad, B. Lowered
     Monoamine Oxidase Activity in Brains from Alcoholic Suicides.
     Journal of Neurochemistry, 25: 667-673, 1975.

445. Gould, L., Reddy, C.V.R., Becker, W., Oh, K.-C. and Kim, S.G.
     Electrophysiologic Properties of Alcohol in Man. Journal
     of Electrocardiology, 11: 219-226, 1978.

446. Gradillas Regodón, Vicente. Alcoholismo en la vejez. [Alcoholism
     in Old Age.] Actas Luso-Espagñolas de Neurologia, Psiquitrua
     y Ciencias Afines, 2(1): 3-14, 1974.

447. Gradillas Regodón, Vicente. Alcoholismo en la vejez. [Alcoholism
     in Old Age.] Actas Luso-Espagñolas de Neurologia, Psiquitrua
     y Ciencias Afines, 5(1): 15-28, 1977.

448. Grahmann, H. and Neumann, H. Pneumoencephalographische Unter-
     suchungen an Trinkern. [Pneumoencephalographic Studies in
     Alcoholics.] Archiv für Psychiatrie und Nervenkrankheiten,
     203: 178-184, 1962.

449. Grant, A.P. and Boyd, M.W.J. An Assessment of the Incidence of
     Chronic Alcoholism in Northern Ireland. British Journal of
     Addiction, 58: 39-44, 1962.

450. Grant, A.P. and Boyd, M.W.J. Chronic Alcoholism: A Survey of
     the Incidence in Downe Hospital Area. Ulster Medical Jour-
     nal, 30: 114-118, 1962.

451. Graux, P. L'alcoolisme des vieillards. [Alcoholism of the Elder-
     ly.] Revue de l'Alcoolisme, 15: 46-48, 1969.

452. Green, A.J. and Ratnoff, O.D. Elevated Antihemophilic Factor
     (AHF, Factor VIII) Procoagulant Activity and AHF-like Anti-
     gen in Alcoholic Cirrhosis of the Liver. Journal of Labora-
     tory and Clinical Medicine, 83: 189-197, 1974.

453. Greenblatt, M., Healey, M.M. and Jones, G.A. Age and Electro-
     encephalographic Abnormality in Neuropsychiatric Patients;
     A Study of 1,593 Cases. American Journal of Psychiatry, 101:
     82-90, 1944.

454. Greenblatt, M., Levin, S. and Di Cori, F. Electroencephalogram Associated with Chronic Alcoholism, Alcoholic Psychosis and Alcoholic Convulsions. Archives of Neurology and Psychiatry, 52: 290-295, 1944.

455. Greffi, E. Alcoolismo e vecchiaia; divagazioni in aperatura di simposio. [Alcoholism and Old Age: Thoughts on the Subject at the Opening of the Symposium.] Giornale di Gerontologia, 15(1): 13-16, 1967.

456. Gregory, I. Factors Influencing First Admission Rates to Canadian Mental Hospitals. I. An Analysis of Trends, 1932-53 (by Age, Sex, Diagnosis and Methods of Admission). Canadian Psychiatric Association Journal, 1: 115-143, 1956.

457. Grosberg, S.J. Lipemia Reinalis, Hyperlipemia, and Hepatosplenomegaly in Chronic Alcoholic Patient. New York State Journal of Medicine, 66: 2951-2953, 1966.

458. Gross, Gilbert. Etude de la longevité chez les malades mentaux. [A study of Longevity in Mental Patients.] Schweizer Archiv für Neurologie, Neurochirurgie und Psychiatrie, 108(1): 125-143, 1971.

459. Gross, Milton M., Rosenblatt, Sidney M., Lewis, Eastlyn, Malenowski, Beverly and Broman, Melinda. Hallucinations and Clouding of Sensorium in Alcohol Withdrawal; Some Demographic and Cultural Relationships. Quarterly Journal of Studies on Alcohol, 32(4): 1061-1069, 1971.

460. Gross, William F. and Nerviano, Vincent J. The Use of the Personality Research Form with Alcoholics: Effects of Age and IQ. Journal of Clinical Psychology, 29(3): 378-379, 1973.

461. Grosso, F. Inchiesta alcoolica: Ricerca e studio clinico statisico su 3009 malati di una Divisione di Medicina Generale. [Alcoholism Survey: Clinicostatisical Study of 3009 Patients in a Department of General Medicine.] Archivio per le Scienze Mediche, 135: 277-287, 1978.

462. Grüneberg, F. Zur Phänomenologie suizidaler Handlungen im höheren Lebensalter. [Phenomenology of Suicidal Action in Old Age.] Aktuelle Gerontologie, 7: 91-100, 1977.

463. Guidi, M. Il quadro proteico e lipidico del siero nella senescenza normale demente arteriosclerotico e nell'alcoolista cronico. [The Protein and Lipid Picture of Blood in Normal Senescence, in the Arteriosclerotic Dement and in the Chronic Alcoholic.] Ospedale Psichiatrico, 31: 237-244, 1963.

464. Guillemant, S., Vitoux, J.-F., Desgrez, P., Saigot, T. and Sarrazin, A. Dosage radio-immunologique de l'arginine-vasopressine plasmatique chez le cirrhotique; quinze malades. [Radioimmunological Determination of Plasma Arginine Vasopressin in Cirrhotics; 15 Cases.] Nouvelle Presse Médicale, 7, 3048-3049, 1978.

465. Gullotta, F. Demyelination of Corpus Callosum in Chronic Alco-
      holism. Marchiafava-Bignami's Disease. Tohoku Journal of
      Experimental Medicine, 72: 201-209, 1960.

466. Guttmann, David. Patterns of Legal Drug Use by Older Americans.
      Addictive Diseases, 3(3): 337-356, 1978.

467. Guttmann, David, Sinnott, Jan D., Carrigan, Zoe H., and Holahan,
      Nancy A. Survey of Drug-Taking Behavior of the Elderly.
      U.S. Department of Health, Education, and Welfare and the
      National Institute of Drug Abuse and the Administration on
      Aging. Rockville, Maryland: NIDA, 1977; Washington, D.C.:
      Catholic University of America, 1977.

H

468. Haberman, Paul W. Denial of Drinking in a Household Survey. Quarterly Journal of Studies on Alcohol, 31: 710-717, 1970.

469. Haberman, Paul W. and Sheinberg, Jill. Implicative Drinking Reported in a Household Survey: A Corroborative Note on Subgroup Differences. Quarterly Journal of Studies on Alcohol, 28(3): 538-543, 1967.

470. Hackney, R.L., Jr. Treating Tuberculosis in the Poor Black Alcoholic Male. American Review of Respiratory Disease, 112: 150-151, 1975.

471. Hackstock, H. Alkoholhalluzinose und Delirium tremens und deren Behandlung mit Vitaminen. [Alcoholic Hallucinosis and Delirium Tremens and Their Treatment with Vitamins.] Therapeutische Umschau, 19: 110-113, 1962.

472. Haddon, William, Jr., Valien, Preston, McCarroll, James R. and Umberger, Charles J. A Controlled Investigation of the Characteristics of Adult Pedestrians Fatally Injured by Motor Vehicles in Manhattan. Journal of Chronic Disease, 14(6): 655-678, 1961.

473. Haglund, R.M.J. and Schuckit, Marc A. Clinical Comparison of Tests of Organicity in Elderly Patients. Journal of Gerontology, 31(6): 654-659, 1976.

474. Hajek, F. and Vojtechovsky, M. Drug Treatment in the First Thirty Days of Hospitalization in the Psychiatric Hospital in Horni Berkovice. Activitas Nervosa Superior, 17(4): 299-300, 1975.

475. Hällen, J. Alkohol och leverskador. [Alcohol and Liver Damage.] Alkoholfragan, 64: 44-48, 1970.

476. Happy-Hour Therapy. Human Behavior, 3(6): 31-32, 1974.

477. Harford, T.C. and Mills, G.S. Age-Related Trends in Alcohol Consumption. Journal of Studies on Alcohol, 39(1): 207-210, 1978.

478. Harrell, H.L., Jr. Long-Term Therapy for the Mental Disturbances
     of Wernicke-Korsakoff Syndrome. Journal of the Florida
     Medical Association, 64(3): 165-167, 1977.

479. Harrington, L. Garth and Price, A. Cooper. Alcoholism in a
     Geriatric Setting. I. Disciplinary Problems, Marital Status
     and Income Level. Journal of the American Geriatrics Soc-
     iety, 10: 197-200, 1962.

480. Harrington, L. Garth and Price, A. Cooper. Alcoholism in a
     Geriatric Setting. II. Education, Military Service, and Em-
     ployment Records. Journal of the American Geriatrics Soc-
     iety, 10: 201-203, 1962.

481. Harrington, L. Garth and Price, A. Cooper. Alcoholism in a
     Geriatric Setting. III. Age on Admission to Domiciliary,
     Length of Stay, Diagnoses, and Source of Income. Journal of
     the American Geriatrics Society, 10: 204-206, 1962.

482. Harrington, L. Garth and Price, A. Cooper. Alcoholism in a
     Geriatric Setting. IV. Incidence of Drug Addiction and
     Disease. Journal of the American Geriatrics Society, 10:
     207-208, 1962.

483. Harrington, L. Garth and Price, A. Cooper. Alcoholism in a
     Geriatric Setting. V. Incidence of Mental Disorders. Jour-
     nal of the American Geriatrics Society, 10: 209-211, 1962.

484. Harris, Louis and Associates, Inc. American Attitudes toward
     Alcohol and Alcoholics: A Survey of Public Opinion.
     Study No. 2138. Prepared for the National Institute on
     Alcohol Abuse and Alcoholism, 1971.

485. Harris, Louis and Associates, Inc. Public Awareness of a NIAAA
     Advertising Campaign and Public Attitudes toward Drinking
     and Alcohol Abuse, Phases One-Four, 1972-74.

486. Hartmann, L., Cornet, A., Barbier, J.-P., Ollier, M.P., Carnot, F.
     and Benisty, H. Réactions immunocytaires de la muqueuse
     gastrique au cours des cirrhoses alcooliques. [Immunocytic
     Reactions of the Gastric Mucosa during Alcoholic Cirrhosis.]
     Semaine des Hôpitaux de Paris, 50: 1559-1566, 1974.

487. Haselager, E.M. and Vreeken, J. Rebound Thrombocytosis after
     Alcohol Abuse: A Possible Factor in the Pathogenesis of
     Thromboembolic Disease. The Lancet, 1: 774-775, 1977.

488. Hasenbush, L. Lee. Successful Brief Therapy of a Retired Elderly
     Man with Intractable Pain, Depression, and Drug and Alcohol
     Dependence. Journal of Geriatric Psychiatry, 10(1): 71-88,
     1977.

489. Hawker, A. Facts and Figures. British Journal of Alcohol and
     Alcoholism, 13: 21-23, 1978.

490. Hayashi, T. and Stemmermann, G.N. Chronic Alcoholism with Pan-
      creatitis, Cirrhosis, and Hyperlipemia; Zieve's Syndrome,
      Report of a Case Studied at Necropsy. Archives of Internal
      Medicine, 120: 465-471, 1967.

491. Hed, R., Nygren, A., Röjdmark, S. and Sundblad, L. Does a Dis-
      turbed Insulin Release Promote Hypoglycemia in Alcoholics?
      Acta Medica Scandinavica, 204: 57-60, 1978.

492. Heikkinen, Eino, Käyhty-Seppänen, Birgit and Pohjolainen, Perrti.
      Health Situation and Related Social Conditions among 66-Year-
      Old Finnish Men. Scandinavian Journal of Social Medicine,
      4: 71-74, 1976.

493. Helderman, J.H., Vestal, R.E., Rowe, J.W., Tobin, J.D., Andres, R.
      and Robertson, G.L. The Response of Arginine Vasopressin to
      Intravenous Ethanol and Hypertonic Saline in Man: The Im-
      pact of Aging. Journal of Gerontology, 33: 39-47, 1978.

494. Hell, D. and Six, P. Thiamin-, Riboflavin- and Pyridoxin-Versor-
      gung bei chronischem Alkoholismus. [Thiamine, Riboflavin,
      and Pyridoxine Supply in Alcoholism.] Deutsche Medizinische
      Wochenschrift, 102: 962-966, 1977.

495. Hell, D. and Six, P. Zur Klinik des Wernicke-Korsakoff-Syndroms.
      [Clinical Aspects of the Wernicke-Korsakoff-Syndrome.]
      Praxis, 65(23): 707-712, 1976.

496. Hell, D., Six, P. and Salkeld, R. Vitamin-B_1-Mangel bei chron-
      ischen Äthylikern und sein klinisches Korrelat. [Vitamin B_1
      Deficiency in Alcoholics and its Clinical Correlate.]
      Schweizerische Medizinische Wochenschrift, 106: 1466-1470,
      1976.

497. Heller, Frank J. and Wynne, Ron. Drug Misuse by the Elderly:
      Indications and Treatment Suggestions. In: Developments
      in the Field of Drug Abuse: Proceedings. Ed. E. Senay,
      V. Shortly, and H. Alksne. Cambridge, Massachusetts:
      Schenkman Pub. Co., 1975, pages 945-955.

498. Helm, S. Use of Cortisone in Laennec's Cirrhosis. Report of a
      Case with Favorable Outcome. Journal of the American Medical
      Association, 151: 383-384, 1953.

499. Henriksen, Jens H. and Winkler, Kjeld. Transvascular Escape Rate
      of Albumin in Liver Cirrhosis, and Its Possible Role in For-
      mation of Ascites. Scandinavian Journal of Gastroenterology,
      12: 877-884, 1977.

500. Hensman, Celia. Problems of Drunkenness amongst Male Recidivists. In: Proceedings of an International Symposium on The Drunkenness Offence held from 15 to 17 May, 1968, at the Institute of Psychiatry, Maudsley Hospital, London, S.E.5. under the Auspices of Camberwell Council on Alcoholism and International Council on Alcohol and Addictions. Ed. Timothy Cook, Dennis Gath, and Celia Hensman. Oxford: Pergamon Press, 1969, pages 35-50, especially pages 38, 44.

501. Herrmann, W.P., Aulepp, H. and Huffmann, G. Lipomatosis symmetrica benigna mit Hyperlipoproteinämie Typ IV und Epipharynx-Karzinom. [Benign Symmetric Lipomatosis with Hyperlipoproteinemia Type IV and Epipharyngeal Carcinoma.] Zeitschrift für Hautkrankheiten, 53: 580-586, 1978.

502. Hewitt, J.M. and Barr, A.M. Premedication with Lorazepam for Bronchoscopy under General Anaesthesia. British Journal of Anaesthesia, 50: 1149-1154, 1978.

503. Hicks, R. Ethanol, a Possible Allergen. Annals of Allergy, 26: 641-643, 1968.

504. Hilden, T. and Svendsen, T.L. Electrolyte Disturbances in Beer Drinkers; a Specific "Hypo-Osmolality Syndrome." The Lancet, 2: 245-246, 1975.

505. Hill, Thomas. Studies Show Seriousness of Alcoholism among Elderly. The Journal, 3(2): 2, 1974.

506. Hillman, Robert W. and Kissin, Benjamin. Oral Cytologic Patterns in Relation to Smoking Habits. Oral Surgery, 42(3): 366-374, 1976.

507. Hirschberg, Besse. Alcoholism in the Case Load of the New York City Welfare Department: A Statistical Analysis. Quarterly Journal of Studies on Alcohol, 15(3): 402-412, 1954.

508. Hirst, A.E., Hadley, G.G. and Gore, I. The Effect of Chronic Alcoholism and Cirrhosis of the Liver on Atherosclerosis. American Journal of Medical Science, 249: 143-149, 1965.

509. Hittel, Z.Z. Perceptual Differentiation among Subtypes of Alcoholics. Ph.D Dissertation, Arizona State University, 1975 (University Microfilms No. 75-22546).

510. Hjortzberg-Nordlund, Hans. Abuse of Alcohol in Middle-Aged Men in Göteborg: A Social Psychiatric Investigation. Acta Psychiatrica Scandinavica, 44 (Supplement 199): 5-127, 1968.

511. Hobson, W., Jordan, A. and Roseman, C. Serum-Cholesterol Levels in Elderly People Living at Home. The Lancet, 265: 961-964, 1953.

512. Hochrein, M. and Schleicher, I. Herz-Kreislaufbeeinflussung durch Alkohol. [Cadiovascular Effects of Alcohol.] Medizinische Klinik, 60: 41-46, 1965.

513. Hochschild, R. Effects of Various Drugs on Longevity in Female
      C57 BL/6J Mice. Gerontologia, 19: 271-280, 1973.

514. Hoffmann, Helmut. Personality Characteristics of Alcoholics
      in Relation to Age. Psychological Reports, 27: 167-171,
      1970.

515. Hoffmann, Helmut. Referral Sources, Prehospital Events and After-
      Care of Young and Old Alcoholics. Willmar St. Hospital,
      pages 1-13, 1970.

516. Hoffmann, Helmut and Nelson, Paul C. Personality Character-
      istics of Alcoholics in Relation to Age and Intelligence.
      Psychological Reports, 29(1): 143-146, 1971.

517. Hoffmann, Helmut and Wefring, Larry R. Sex and Age Differences
      in Psychiatric Symptoms of Alcoholics. Psychological
      Reports, 30: 887-889, 1972.

518. Horie, A., Kotoo, Y. and Nishihara, Y. Histopathological Findings
      of the Pancreas in the Aged and Alcoholics. Nippon Ronen
      Igakkai Zasshi, 14(6): 468-474, 1977.

519. Hornstra, Robijn K. and Udell, Bess. Psychiatric Services and
      Alcoholics. Missouri Medicine, 70(2): 103-107, 1973.

520. Hossack, D.W. and Brown, G. The Hard Facts of the Influence of
      Alcohol on Serious Road Accident Casualties. Medical
      Journal of Australia, 61: 473-479, 1974.

521. Hotson, J.R. and Langston, J.W. Disulfiram-Induced Encephalopa-
      thy. Archives of Neurology, 33: 141-142, 1976.

522. Hubbard, Richard W., Santos, John F. and Santos, Mary Alice.
      Alcohol and Older Adults: Overt and Covert Influences.
      Social Casework: The Journal of Contemporary Social Work,
      60(3): 166-170, 1979.

523. Huckman, Michael S., Fox, Jacob H. and Ramsey, Ruth G. Computed
      Tomography in the Diagnosis of Degenerative Diseases of the
      Brain. Seminars in Roentgenology, 12(1): 63-75, 1977.

524. Hugues, J.N., Perret, G., Adessi, G., Coste, T. and Modigliani, E.
      Effects of Chronic Alcoholism on the Pituitary-Gonadal Func-
      tion of Women during Menopausal Transition and in the Post
      Menopausal Period. Biomedicine, 29: 279-283, 1978.

525. Humphery, T.J. Methanol Poisoning: Management of Acidosis with
      Combined Haemodialysis and Peritoneal Dialysis. Medical
      Journal of Australia, 61: 833-835, 1974.

526. Hunter, A. Longevity and Mortality as Affected by the Use of Al-
      cohol. In: Alcohol and Man. Ed. H.A. Emerson. New York:
      Macmillan, 1932, Chapter 13, pages 327-344.

527. Hutson, D.G., Zeppa, R., Levi, J.U., Schiff, E.R., Livingstone,
      A.S. and Fink, P. The Effect of the Distal Splenorenal Shunt
      on Hypersplenism. Annals of Surgery, 185(5): 605-612, 1977.

528. Hyde, R.W. Alcohol and Geriatrics. Paper presented at G.W.A.N.
      Conference, Sugarbush, October 1971.

529. Hyman, Merton M. Accident Vulnerability and Blood Alcohol Con-
      centrations of Drivers by Demographic Characteristics.
      Quarterly Journal of Studies on Alcohol (Supplement 4):
      34-57, 1968.

530. Hyman, Merton M. Alcoholics 15 Years Later. Annals of the
      New York Academy of Sciences, 273: 613-623, 1976.

531. Hyman, Merton M. The Social Characteristics of Persons Arrested
      for Driving while Intoxicated. Quarterly Journal of Studies
      on Alcohol (Supplement 4): 138-177, 1968.

I

532. Ikeda, H. Serum Creatine Phosphokinase Activity in Newly Admitted
      Chronic Alcoholics. Folia Psychiatrica et Neurologica Japon-
      ica, 31: 9-16, 1977.

533. Ikeda, H., Rassouli, M.E., Fukui, H. and Chuda, M. Hypokalemic
      Myopathy Associated with Chronic Alcoholism. Clinical
      Neurology, 17: 67-73, 1977.

534. Inciardi, James A., McBride, Duane C., Russe, Brian R. and
      Wells, Karen S. Acute Drug Reactions among the Aged: A
      Research Note. Addictive Diseases, 3(3): 383-388, 1978.

535. Ipsen, Johannes, Moore, Merrill and Alexander, Leo. Prevalence
      of Alcoholism in the Population and among Suicides and Acci-
      dents from Poisoning, Massachusetts 1938-1948. Quarterly
      Journal of Studies on Alcohol, 13(2): 204-214, 1952.

536. Isaacs, B., Livingstone, M. and Neville, Y. Survival of the Un-
      fittest: A Study of Geriatric Patients in Glasgow. London:
      Routledge and Kegan Paul, 1972.

537. Isaacson, C. The Changing Pattern of Liver Disease in South
      African Blacks. South African Medical Journal, 53(10):
      365-368, 1978.

538. Ishino, H., Suwaki, H. and Itoshima, T. Liver Function Tests in
      Addictive Alcoholics. Japanese Journal of Studies on Alco-
      hol, 9: 65-72, 1974.

539. Ivy, Andrew C. Alcohol and Longevity, Mortality, and Morbidity.
      In: Toward Prevention: Scientific Studies on Alcohol and
      Alcoholism. Ed. Francis A. Soper. Washington, D.C.: Pub-
      lished for the International Commission for the Prevention of
      Alcoholism by Narcotics Education, Inc., 1971, pages 69-75.

J

540. Jacobs, D.S., Robinson, R.A., Clark, G.M. and Tucker, J.M. Clinical Significance of the Isomorphic Pattern of the Isoenzymes of Serum Lactate Dehydrogenase. Annals of Clinical Laboratory Science, 7(5): 411-421, 1977.

541. Jankelson, O.M., Vitale, J.J. and Hegsted, D.M. Serum Magnesium, Cholesterol and Lipoproteins in Patients with Atherosclerosis and Alcoholism; Some Preliminary Observations. American Journal of Clinical Nutrition, 7: 23-29, 1959.

542. Jansen, D.G. Use of the Personal Orientation Inventory with State Hospital Alcoholics. Journal of Clinical Psychology, 30: 310-311, 1974.

543. Jarvis, G.K. Mormon Mortality Rates in Canada. Social Biology, 24: 294-302, 1977.

544. Jellinek, E. Morton. "Death from Alcoholism" in the United States in 1940: A Statistical Analysis. Quarterly Journal of Studies on Alcohol, 3(3): 465-494, 1942.

545. Jellinek, E. Morton. Notes on the First Half Year's Experience at the Yale Plan Clinics. Quarterly Journal of Studies on Alcohol, 5(2): 279-302, 1944-45.

546. Jellinek, E. Morton. Phases in the Drinking History of Alcoholics: Analysis of a Survey Conducted by the Official Organ of Alcoholics Anonymous. Quarterly Journal of Studies on Alcohol, 7(1): 1-88, 1946.

547. Jellinek, E. Morton. Recent Trends in Alcoholism and in Alcohol Consumption. Quarterly Journal of Studies on Alcohol, 8(1): 1-42, 1947-48.

548. Johannes, K. and Giovanardi, F. L'alcoolismo nell'eta senile (La patologia in genere nel bevitore anziano). [Alcoholism in the Elderly (General Pathology in the Aged Drinker.)] Giornale di Gerontologia, 15(1): 136-144, 1967.

549. Johansen, K. and Theilade, P. Alkoholisk ketoacidose. [Alco-
          holic Ketoacidosis.] Ugeskrift for Laeger, 140: 226-228,
          1978.

550. Johansson, R., Oom, J. and Sjöberg, C. Alkoholen i medicinen.
          (Alcohol in Medicine.] Läkartidningen, 75: 1809-1810, 1978.

551. Johnson, G.F. and Leeman, M.M. Analysis of Familial Factors in
          Bipolar Affective Illness. Archives of General Psychiatry,
          34(9): 1074-1083, 1977.

552. Johnson, Laverne C. Sleep Patterns in Chronic Alcoholics. In:
          Recent Advances in Studies of Alcoholism: An Interdisci-
          plinary Symposium. Ed. Nancy K. Mello and Jack H. Mendel-
          son. Publication No. (HSM) 71-9045. Washington, D.C.:
          U.S. Government Printing Office, 1971.

553. Johnson, Louise A. and Goodrich, Charles H. Use of Alcohol by
          Persons 65 Years and Over, Upper East Side of Manhattan.
          Final Report Submitted to the National Institute on Alcohol
          Abuse and Alcoholism, under Contract #HSM-43-73-38-NIA,
          January 1974. New York: Mount Sinai School of Medicine,
          1974. Springfield, Virginia: NTIS, 1974.

554. Johnson, Paula, Armor, David J., Polich, Suzanne and Stambul, Har-
          riet. U.S. Adult Drinking Practices: Time Trends, Social
          Correlates and Sex Roles. (A Working Note prepared for the
          National Institute on Alcohol Abuse and Alcoholism.) San-
          ta Monica, California: Rand Corporation, 1977.

555. Johnson, W.M., ed. The Older Patient. New York: Paul B. Hoeker,
          1960.

556. Johnston, W.D. and Ballantyne, A.J. Prognostic Effect of Tobacco
          and Alcohol Use in Patients with Oral Tongue Cancer. (Scien-
          tific Papers.) American Journal of Surgery, 134: 444-447,
          1977.

557. Jones, B. and Parsons, O.A. Impaired Abstracting Ability in
          Chronic Alcoholics. Archives of General Psychiatry, 24:
          71-75, 1971.

558. Jones, B. and Parsons, O.A. Specific vs. Generalized Deficits of
          Abstracting Ability in Chronic Alcoholics. Archives of
          General Psychiatry, 26: 380-384, 1972.

559. Jones, B.P., Moskowitz, H.R., Butters, Nelson and Glosser, G.
          Psychophysical Scaling of Olfactory, Visual and Auditory
          Stimuli by Alcoholic Korsakoff Patients. Neuropsychologia,
          13: 387-393, 1975.

560. Jones, E.W. Patient Classification for Long-Term Care: User's
          Manual. DHEW Publication No. HRA 75-3107. Washington, D.C.:
          Government Printing Office, 1974.

561. Jones, R.E. A Study of 100 Physician Psychiatric Inpatients.
      American Journal of Psychiatry, 134(10): 1119-1123, 1977.

562. Jorke, D. and Reinhardt, M. Epidemiology of Chronic Liver
      Diseases. Acta Hepato-Gastroenterologica, 24: 220-225, 1977.

563. Josserand, A. and Lejeune, E. De l'influence aggravante de
      l'éthylisme sur l'évolution des épithéliomas buccopharyngés.
      [The Aggravating Effect of Alcoholism on the Evolution of
      Buccopharyngeal Epitheliomas.] Lyon Médical, 184: 165-166,
      1951.

564. Jost, F. and Geertz, U.W. Modernos tratamientos en psiquiatriá
      curas de deshabituacion: El problema maníaco, el alcoholis-
      mo crónico y su tratamiento. [Modern Treatments in the Psy-
      chiatric Cure of Withdrawal: The Mania Problem, Chronic
      Alcoholism, and Its Treatment.] Folia Clinica Internacional,
      11(9): 495-505, 1961.

565. Jost, F. and Geertz, U.W. Problema maníaco y alcoholismo crónico,
      afecciones psiquiatricas en la edad involutiva. [The Mania
      Problem and Chronic Alcoholism, Psychiatric Disorders during
      Menopause.] Folia Clinica Internacional, 11(10): 538-546,
      1961.

566. Junod, B. and Pasche, R. Etio-épidémiologie des cancers de la
      bouche et du pharynx en Suisse. [Etio-epidemiology of Mouth
      and Pharyngeal Cancers in Switzerland.] Schweizerische
      Medizinische Wochenschrift, 108(24): 882-887, 1978.

567. Justin-Besançon, L., Durand, H., Dorfmann, H., Gueroult, N.,
      Voisin, P.M., Roge, J. and Etienne, J.P. Survie des cir-
      rhoses alcooliques ascitiques: Comparaison des résultats
      de trois enquêtes faites sur une période de vingt ans. [The
      Survival Rate of Ascitic Alcoholic Cirrhosis Patients: Com-
      parison of the Results of Three Surveys Made over a Period
      of Twenty Years.] Annales Médecine Interne, 122(1): 49-54,
      1971.

568. Justin-Besançon, L., Klotz, H.P., Pluvinage, R. and Villiaumey, J.
      Ophtalmoplégie brutale chez une éthylique. Syndrome de Wer-
      nicke. Guérison par l'aneurine. [Sudden Ophthalmoplegia in
      an Alcoholic Woman. Wernicke's Syndrome. Recovery with
      Aneurin.] Bulletin et Mémoires de la Société Médicale des
      Hôpitaux de Paris, 65: 1419-1422, 1949.

K

569. Kahn, Alfred J. Changes in Ethanol Consumption by C3H and CFl Mice with Age. Journal of Studies on Alcohol, 36(9): 1107-1123, 1975.

570. Kahn, Alfred J. Delay of Development of Responses to Ethanol in Mice; Associated Delay in Another Parameter. Journal of Studies on Alcohol, 38(1): 39-46, 1977.

571. Kahn, Alfred J. Site Selection and the Response to Ethanol in C3H Mice; Passive Acceptance versus Active Attraction. Quarterly Journal of Studies on Alcohol, 30(3): 609-617, 1969.

572. Kakihana, R. and McClearn, G.E. Development of Alcohol Preference in BALB/c Mice. Nature, 199: 511-512, 1963.

573. Kapp, F. and Buess, H.J. Ösophaguswandsklerosierung als Therapie blutender Ösophagusvarizen bei inoperablen Patienten; vergleichende Resultate bei 14 behandelten und 14 unbehandelten Patienten. [Sclerosing of Esophageal Walls as a Treatment of Bleeding Esophageal Varices in Inoperable Patients; Comparative Results of 14 Treated and 14 Untreated Patients.] Deutsche Medizinische Wochenschrift, 98: 2465-2469, 1973.

574. Kapur, N. Visual Imagery Capacity of Alcohol Korsakoff Patients. Neuropsychologia, 16(4): 517-519, 1978.

575. Karp, S.A. and Konstadt, N.L. Alcoholism and Psychological Differentiation: Long-Range Effects of Heavy Drinking on Field Dependence. Journal of Nervous and Mental Disease, 140: 412-416, 1965.

576. Kárpáti, M., Annau, V. and Orthmayr, A. Pneumographiás elváltozások alkoholistaknal. [Pneumoencephalographic Changes in Alcoholics.] In: Tanulmányok az alkoholizmus pszichiátriai következményeiröl. [Results of Psychiatric Study of Alcoholism.] Ed. I. Tariska, G. Geréby, and G. Kardos. Budapest: Alkoholizmus Elleni Orszagos Bizottsag, 1969, pages 99-105.

577. Kastenbaum, Robert. Beer, Wine, and Mutual Gratification in
        the Gerontopolis. In: Research Planning and Action for
        the Elderly: The Power and Potential of Social Science.
        Ed. Donald P. Kent, Robert Kastenbaum, and Sylvia Sherwood.
        New York: Behavioral Publications, 1972, pages 365-394.

578. Kastenbaum, Robert. Wine and Fellowship in Aging: An Exploratory
        Action Program. Journal of Human Relations, 13(2): 266-275,
        1965.

579. Kastenbaum, Robert. Wine, Psyche, and the Aged. Phase I. Final
        Report. Boston, Massachusetts: Unpublished report, 1973.

580. Kastenbaum, Robert, Sarley, V.C. and Stepto, R.C. The Use of
        Wine in Hospitals and Nursing Homes; a Panel Discussion.
        In: Wine and Health (Proceedings of the First International
        Symposium on Wine and Health held at the University of Chi-
        cago Center for Continuing Education, 9 November 1968).
        Ed. Salvatore P. Lucia. Menlo Park, California: Pacific
        Coast Publishers, 1969, pages 23-32.

581. Kastenbaum, Robert and Simon, W. Wine and Morale in the Rehab-
        ilitation of Elderly Patients. Unpublished manuscript.
        Framingham, Massachusetts: Cushing Hospital, 1964.

582. Kastenbaum, Robert and Slater, Philip E. Effects of Wine on the
        Interpersonal Behavior of Geriatric Patients: An Exploratory
        Study. In: New Thoughts on Old Age. Ed. Robert Kasten-
        baum. New York: Springer Publishing Co., 1964, pages 191-
        204.

583. Kayne, R.C., ed. Drugs and the Elderly. Rev. ed. Los Angeles,
        California: University of Southern California Press, 1978.

584. Keen, R.I. Blood Alcohol Levels: A Survey of Four Months in
        Manchester. Medicine, Science, and the Law, 8: 150-152,
        1968.

585. Keil, Thomas J. Sex Role Variations and Women's Drinking: Re-
        sults from a Household Survey in Pennsylvania. Journal of
        Studies on Alcohol, 39(5): 859-868, 1978.

586. Keiser, G. and Beck, D. Alkoholanämie. [Alcohol Anemia.]
        Praxis, 55: 598-604, 1966.

587. Keller, Andrew Z. Alcohol, Tobacco and Age Factors in the Rela-
        tive Frequency of Cancer among Males with and without Liver
        Cirrhosis. American Journal of Epidemiology, 106(3): 194-
        202, 1977.

588. Keller, Andrew Z. Liver Cirrhosis, Tobacco, Alcohol and Cancer
        among Blacks. Journal of the National Medical Association,
        70: 575-580, 1978.

589. Kellner, K. Ein Fall von Antabus-Vergiftung. [A Case of Antabus
        Poisoning.] Medizinische Klinik, 48: 1034-1036, 1953.

590. Kern, J.C., Schmelter, W.R. and Paul, S.R. Drinking Drivers Who
      Complete and Drop Out of an Alcohol Education Program. Jour-
      nal of Studies on Alcohol, 38(1): 89-95, 1977.

591. Kessel, N. and Grossman, G. Suicide in Alcoholics. British Medi-
      cal Journal, 2: 1671-1672, 1961.

592. Khan, J.S., Wilson, M.C. and Taylor, T.V. A Case of Dettol
      Addiction. British Medical Journal, 1: 791-792, 1979.

593. Khantzian, E.J. Organic Problems in the Aged--Brain Syndromes
      and Alcoholism; Nature of the Dependency and Denial Problems
      of Alcoholics. Journal of Geriatric Psychiatry, 11(2): 191-
      202, 1978.

594. Khoo, O.T. and Fernandez, P. The Problem of Alcoholism in Singa-
      pore. Singapore Medical Journal, 12: 154-160, 1971.

595. Kiessling, K.-H., Pilström, L., Karlsson, J. and Piehl, Karin.
      Mitochondrial Volume in Skeletal Muscle from Young and Old
      Physically Untrained and Trained Healthy Men and from Alco-
      holics. Clinical Science, 44(6): 547-554, 1973.

596. King, A.P. Cocktail Hour in a Nursing Home. Nursing Care, 10(2):
      26, 1977.

597. King, W.E. and Perry, J.W. Liver Changes in Alcoholism Studied
      by Aspiration of the Liver, with Report of a Case. Royal
      Melbourne Hospital Clinic Report, 18: 71-73, 1947.

598. Kinney, J. and Leaton, G. The Elderly. In: Loosening the Grip;
      A Handbook of Alcohol Information. St. Louis, Missouri:
      C.V. Mosby Co., 1978, pages 228-241.

599. Kirkpatrick, J.B. and Pearson, J. Fatal Cerebral Injury in the
      Elderly. Journal of the American Geriatrics Society, 26:
      489-497, 1978.

600. Kirshbaum, J.D. and Shure, N. Alcoholic Cirrhosis of the Liver:
      A Clinical and Pathologic Study of 356 Fatal Cases Selected
      from 12,267 Necropsies. Journal of Laboratory and Clinical
      Medicine, 28: 721-731, 1943.

601. Kissin, Benjamin, Platz, Arthur and Su, Wen Huey. Selective
      Factors in Treatment Choice and Outcome in Alcoholics. In:
      Recent Advances in Studies of Alcoholism: An Interdisci-
      plinary Symposium. Ed. Nancy K. Mello and Jack H. Mendelson.
      Publication No. (HSM) 71-9045. Washington, D.C.: U.S. Gov-
      ernment Printing Office, 1971.

602. Kittredge, L.D., Franklin, J.L., Thrasher, J.H. and Berdiansky,
      H.A. Estimating a Population in Need of Alcoholism Services:
      A New Approach. International Journal of Addiction, 12(2-3):
      205-226, 1977.

603. Kjølstad, H. Vernehjemmets funksjon i alkoholistomsorgen. [The
     Function of a Protective Home in the Care of Alcoholics.]
     Tidsskrift om Edruskaps Spørsmal, 29(4): 10-11, 1977.

604. Klassen, Deidre and Hornstra, Robijn K. Prevalence of Problem
     Drinking in a Community Survey. Missouri Medicine, 73: 81-84,
     1976.

605. Klatsky, A.L., Friedman, G.D. and Siegelaub, A.B. Alcohol Use,
     Myocardial Infarction, Sudden Cardiac Death, and Hypertension.
     Alcoholism, 3(1): 33-39, 1979.

606. Klatsky, A.L., Friedman, G.D., Siegelaub, A.B. and Gerard, M.J.
     Alcohol Consumption among White, Black, or Oriental Men and
     Women: Kaiser-Permanente Multiphasic Health Examination
     Data. American Journal of Epidemiology, 105(4): 311-323,
     1977.

607. Kleinknecht, Ronald A. and Goldstein, Steven G. Neuropsychologi-
     cal Deficits Associated with Alcoholism: A Review and Dis-
     cussion. Quarterly Journal of Studies on Alcohol, 33: 999-
     1019, 1972.

608. Klemm, Harmut. Der chronische Alkoholismus im Alter. [The
     Chronic Alcoholic in the Aged.] Proceedings of the Seventh
     International Congress of Gerontology, Vienna. Wiener Medi-
     zinischen Akademie, 3: 51-54, 1966.

609. Klewin, K.M., Appen, R.E. and Kaufman, P.L. Amaurosis and Blood
     Loss. American Journal of Ophthalmology, 86: 669-672, 1978.

610. Klisz, Diane K. and Parsons, Oscar A. Hypothesis Testing in
     Younger and Older Alcoholics. Journal of Studies on Alcohol,
     38(9): 1718-1729, 1977.

611. Klotz, U., Avant, G.R., Hoyumpa, A., Schenker, S. and Wilkinson,
     G.R. The Effects of Age and Liver Disease on the Disposi-
     tion and Elimination of Diazepam in Adult Man. Journal of
     Clinical Investigation, 55: 347-359, 1975.

612. Knox, Wilma J. Four-Year Follow-Up of Veterans Treated on a
     Small Alcoholism Treatment Ward. Quarterly Journal of
     Studies on Alcohol, 33(1): 105-110, 1972.

613. Knupfer, Genevieve and Room, Robin. Abstainers in a Metropolitan
     Community. Quarterly Journal of Studies on Alcohol, 31(1):
     108-131, 1970.

614. Knupfer, Genevieve and Room, Robin. Age, Sex, and Social Class
     as Factors in Amount of Drinking in a Metropolitan Community.
     Social Problems, 12: 224-240, 1964.

615. Knutsen, B. Komplikasjoner ved Antabus-Behandlung. [Complica-
     tions in Treatment with Antabus.] Tidsskrift for den Norske
     Laegeforening, 69: 436-437, 1949.

616. Koff, R.S., Bell, B. and Garvey, A.J.   Hearing Levels in a Normal
      Veteran Population: Relationship to Alcohol Consumption.
      Digestion, 9: 36-40, 1973.

617. Kollerits, I. and Bálint, I.   Alkoholista betegek haláloki ada-
      tainak vizsgálata.   [Study of the Causes of Death in Alco-
      holic Patients.]   Alkohológia, 2: 143-147, 1971.

618. Kolotilin, G.F.   Psikhopatologiia alkogol'nogo deliriia s let-
      al'num iskhodom.   [The Psychopathology of Alcoholic Delirium
      with Fatal Outcome.]   Zhurnal Nevropatologii i Psikhiatrii
      Imeni S.S. Korsakova, 74: 240-243, 1974.

619. Komura, S., Ueda, M. and Kobayashi, T.   A Successful Method for
      Development of Voluntary Alcohol Intoxication in Mice.
      Tohoku Journal of Experimental Medicine, 188: 173-179, 1976.

620. Koranyi, E.K.   Fatalities in 2,070 Psychiatric Outpatients.   Ar-
      chives of General Psychiatry, 34(10): 1137-1142, 1977.

621. Korboot, Paula J. and Naylor, G.F.K.   Patterns of WAIS and MIA
      in Alcoholic Dementia.   Australian Journal of Psychology,
      24(2): 227-234, 1972.

622. Korboot, Paula J., Naylor, G.F.K. and Soares, A.   Patterns of
      Cognitive Dysfunction in Alcoholics.   Australian Journal of
      Psychology, 29(1): 25-30, 1977.

623. Krasilowsky, D., Halpern, B. and Gutman, I.   The Problem of Alco-
      holism in Israel.   Israel Annals of Psychiatry and Related
      Disciplines, 3: 249-258, 1965.

624. Krasner, N., Davis, M., Portmann, B. and Williams, R.   Changing
      Pattern of Alcoholic Liver Disease in Great Britain: Re-
      ʼlation to Sex and Signs of Autoimmunity.   British Medical
      Journal, 1: 1497-1500, 1977.

625. Kraus, J.   Alcoholism and Drug Dependence as Factors in Psychia-
      tric Hospital Admissions.   Australian and New Zealand Jour-
      nal of Psychiatry, 7: 45-50, 1973.

626. Kraus, Jess F., D'Ambrosia, Robert D., Smith, Elmore G., Van Met-
      er, Jerry, Borhani, Nemat O., Franti, Charles E. and Lips-
      comb, Paul R.   An Epidemiological Study of Severe Osteoarth-
      ritis.   Orthopedics, 1(1): 37-42, 1978.

627. Krupka, Lawrence R. and Vener, Arthur M.   Hazards of Drug Use
      among the Elderly.   Gerontologist, 19(1): 90-95, 1979.

628. Kuller, L.H., Kramer, K. and Fisher, R.   Changing Trends in Cir-
      rhosis and Fatty Liver Mortality.   American Journal of Pub-
      lic Health, 59: 1124-1133, 1969.

629. Kuller, L.H., Perper, J.A., Cooper, M. and Fisher, R.   An Epi-
      demic of Deaths Attributed to Fatty Liver in Baltimore.
      Preventive Medicine, 3: 61-79, 1974.

630. Kürzinger. Richard. Der Alkoholabbau bei alten Menschen. [Metab-
      olism of Alcohol in Old Persons.] Deutsche Gesundheitswesen,
      18: 1224-1230, 1963.

631. Kürzinger, Richard. Zum klinischen Bild der Alkoholbeeinflussung
      bei alten Menschen. [The Clinical Picture of the Effect of
      Alcohol in Old Persons.] Zeitschrift für Alternsforschung,
      17(1): 1-14, 1963.

L

632. Labrune, M., Dayras, M., Kalifa, G. and Rey, J.L. "Le poumon du cirrhotique," une nouvelle entité radiologique? A propos de 182 observations. ["Cirrhotic's Lung," a New Radiological Entity? Concerning 182 Cases.] Journal de Radiologie et d'Electrologie, 57: 471-475, 1976.

633. Laessig, R.H. and Waterworth, K.J. Involvement of Alcohol in Fatalities of Wisconsin Drivers. Public Health Report, 85: 535-549, 1970.

634. Lagerspetz, K.Y.H. Postnatal Development of the Effects of Alcohol and of the Induced Tolerance to Alcohol in Mice. Acta Pharmacologica et Toxicologica, 31: 497-508, 1972.

635. Lairy, G.C., Goldsteinas, L. and Guennoc, A. Les troubles du sommeil chez les malades présentant des syndromes confusionnels et dementiels. [Sleep Disorders in Patients Presenting Confusional and Demential Syndromes.] Revue Neurologique, 115: 498-507, 1966.

636. L'alcoolisme des personnes âgées: Conclusions et voeux (Colloque du Groupement Médical d'Etude sur l'Alcoolisme). [Alcoholism in Aged Persons: Conclusions and Proposals (Colloquium of the Medical Group on the Study of Alcoholism).] Revue de l'Alcoolisme, 15: 64-65, 1969.

637. Lamarche, A., Davoste, Chuberre and Delelande. La sénilité précoce des alcooliques. [Early Senility of Alcoholics.] Echo Médical du Nord, 23(5): 1, 8, 1952. (Also in: Bulletin de l'Academie Nationale de Médecine, 136: 31-33, 1952.)

638. Lammers, W. De invloed van leeftijd op de reactie van het lichaam op geneesmiddelen. [The Effect of Aging on the Reaction of the Body to Drugs.] Nederlands Tijdschrift voor Geneeskunde, 121(42): 1656-1658, 1977.

639. Lamy, J., Lamy, J., Aron, E. and Weill, J. Profil biologique des premières étapes de la cirrhose alcoolique: IgA, transferrine, haptoglobine, orosomucoide et α_1-antitrypsine. [Biological Profile in Early Stages of Alcoholic Liver Cirrhosis: IgA, Transferrin, Haptoglobin, Orosomucoid, and α_1-antitrypsin.] Pathologie Biologie, 22: 401-408, 1974.

640. Lamy, Peter P. Therapeutics and the Elderly. Addictive Diseases, 3(3): 311-335, 1978.

641. Lance, J.W. Familial Paroxysmal Dystonic Choreoathetosis and Its Differentiation from Related Syndromes. Annals of Neurology, 2(4): 285-293, 1977.

642. Landis, C. and Farwell, J.E. A Trend Analysis of Age at First-Admission, Age at Death, and Years of Residence for State Mental Hospitals: 1913-1941. Journal of Abnormal and Social Psychology, 39: 3-23, 1944.

643. Langer, Gerhard, Heinze, Gerhard, Reim, Beatrix and Matussek, Norbert. Reduced Growth Hormone Responses to Amphetamine in "Endogenous" Depressive Patients: Studies in Normal, "Reactive" and "Endogenous" Depressive, Schizophrenic, and Chronic Alcoholic Subjects. Archives of General Psychiatry, 33(12): 1471-1475, 1976.

644. Lao, B. Zmiany narządowe w przewlekłym alkoholizmie. [Organic Changes in Chronic Alcoholism.] Polski Tygodnik Lekarski, 33: 743-745, 1978.

645. Larsen, Anne, Sivertsen, Egil and Semb, Gudmund. Immediate and Late Results of Aortic Valve Replacement with the Bjőrk-Shiley Tilting Disc Valve. Scandinavian Journal of Thoracic and Cardiovascular Surgery, 12(3): 189-196, 1978.

646. Lasagna, Louis. Drug Effects as Modified by Aging. In: The Neurologic and Psychiatric Aspects of the Disorders of Aging. Ed. J. Moore, H. Merritt, and R. Massilink. Baltimore, Maryland: The Williams and Wilkins Company, 1956, pages 83-94. (Also in Journal of Chronic Diseases, 3: 567-574, 1956.)

647. Lasserre, O., Flamant, R., Lellouch, J. and Schwartz, D. Alcool et cancer; étude de pathologie geographique portant sur les départements français. [Alcohol and Cancer; Study of Geographic Pathology Carried Out in the French Departments.] Bulletin de l'Institut National de la Santé et de la Recherche Médicale, 22: 53-60, 1957.

648. Laube, H., Norris, H.T. and Robbins, S.L. The Nephromegaly of Chronic Alcoholics with Liver Disease. Archives of Pathology, 84: 290-294, 1967.

649. Lauterburg, F. Sterbehäufigkeit und Todesalter bei Alkoholkranken. [Mortality and Age at Death of Alcoholic Patients.] Gesundheit und Wohlfahrt, 25: 574-1945.

650. Leach, Barry. Does Alcoholics Anonymous Really Work? In: Alcoholism: Progress in Research and Treatment. Ed. Peter G. Bourne and Ruth Fox. New York and London: Academic Press, 1973, Chapter 11, Part 6 (Comparison of 4 AA Studies), pages 262-266, especially pages 265-266.

651. Leaf, Alexander. Every Day Is a Gift When You Are Over 100. National Geographic, 93-118, 1973.

652. Leake, Chauncey D. On the Enjoyment of Life and the Process of Aging. In: The Crisis in Health Care for the Aging. Ed. Leon Summit. New York: National Conference of the Huxley Institute for Biosocial Research, March 6, 1972.

653. Leake, Chauncey D. and Silverman, Milton. The Clinical Use of Wine in Geriatrics. Geriatrics, 22: 175-180, 1967.

654. LeBoeuf, A., Lodge, J. and Eames, P.G. Vasopressin and Memory in Korsakoff Syndrome. The Lancet, 2: 1370, 1978.

655. Lecompte, J.M., Goudemand, M., Tauziède-Castel, C., Tabet, C., Weiss, D., Caridroit, M. and Fontan, M. La confrontation des examens biologiques dans l'alcoolisme chronique; une etude statistique chez 103 sujets. [Comparison of Biological Examinations in Chronic Alcoholism; Statistical Study of 103 Patients.] Lille Médicale, 23(2): 80-87, 1978.

656. Ledermann, Sully. Mortalité et alcoolisation excessive. [Mortality and Excessive Alcoholism.] Société de Statistique de Paris, Journal, 99: 28-42, 1958.

657. Lee, K. Alkoholisk cerebellar kortikal atrofi. [Alcoholic Cerebellar Cortical Atrophy.] Ugeskrift for Laeger, 140: 2651-2652, 1978.

658. Lee, Peter V. Drug Therapy in the Elderly: The Clinical Pharmacology of Aging. Alcoholism: Clinical and Experimental Research, 2(1): 39-42, 1978.

659. Lefft, H.H. Some Nutritional and Therapeutic Aspects of Wine and Cognac. International Record of Medicine, 170: 361-368, 1957.

660. Leibetseder, F. Akute thrombopenische Purpura nach Antabusbehandlung. [Acute Thrombopenic Purpura after Treatment with Antabus.] Wiener Klinische Wochenschrift, 64: 431-432, 1952.

661. Lemere, F. What Happens to Alcoholics. American Journal of Psychiatry, 109: 674-676, 1953.

662. Lennon, Beatrice E., Rekosh, Jerold H., Patch, Vernon D. and Howe, Louisa P. Self-Reports of Drunkenness Arrests: Assessing Drinking Problems among Men Hospitalized for Tuberculosis. Quarterly Journal of Studies on Alcohol, 31(1): 90-96, 1970.

663. Leopold, D. Alkoholdelikte und Lebensalter. [Alcohol-Related
      Crimes and Age.] Alcoholism, 10(12): 3-12, 1974.

664. Le-Quang, N.-T., Tenaillon, A., Jacquot, C., Dubrisay, J. and
      Lissac, J. Lactacidémie et pyruvicémie à l'effort dans
      les cirrhoses decompensées. [Lactacidemia and Pyruvemia
      Following Stress in Decompensated Cirrhosis.] Nouvelle
      Presse Médicale, 7: 3555-3556, 1978.

665. Lerche, E., Andre, J.-M. and Voiment, Y.-M. Ascites cirrhotiques:
      Traitement par dérivation péritonéo-veineuse de Le Veen.
      [Ascites Due to Cirrhosis: Treatment by Le Veen's Peritoneo-
      Venous Shunt.] Nouvelle Presse Médicale, 7: 3458-3459, 1978.

666. Lereboullet, J. L'espérance da vie des alcooliques. [Life Ex-
      pectancy of Alcoholics.] Revue de l'Alcoolisme, 14: 279-
      289, 1968.

667. Levenson, Julia. Treatment Concept for the Older Alcoholic.
      Washington, D.C.: NCA Forum (NCAII), May 1976.

668. Levin, D.C., Schwarz, M.I., Matthay, R.A. and Laforce, F.M.
      Bacteremic Hemophilus Influenzae Pneumonia in Adults: A
      Report of 24 Cases and a Review of the Literature. American
      Journal of Medicine, 62(2): 219-224, 1977.

669. Levine, M.L. Cimetidine-Induced Coma in Cirrhosis of the Liver
      Journal of the American Medical Association, 240: 1238,
      1978.

670. Lewis, T.D. Complications of Chronic Pancreatitis. Australian
      and New Zealand Journal of Medicine, 4: 518-521, 1974.

671. Lian, Chen Fah and Robinson, Arvin Edward. Atypical Radiographic
      Appearance and Clinical Presentation of Pulmonary Tuberculo-
      sis. Southern Medical Journal, 69(10): 1317-1322, 1976.

672. Lieber, C.S. and Decarli, L.M. Hepatic Microsomal Ethanol-Oxi-
      dizing System; in Vitro Characteristics and Adaptive Proper-
      ties in Vivo. Journal of Biological Chemistry, 245: 2505-
      2512, 1970.

673. Lifshitz, Kenneth and Kline, Nathan S. Psychopharmacology
      of the Aged. In: Clinical Principles and Drugs in the
      Aging. Ed. Joseph T. Freeman. Springfield, Illinois:
      Charles C. Thomas, 1963, pages 421-457.

674. Linck, K. Alter, letale Dosis und Blutalkoholbefunde bei der
      tödlichen Aethylalkoholvergiftung. [Age, Lethal Dosage
      and Blood Alcohol in Fatal Ethyl Alcohol Poisoning.] Medi-
      zinische Klinik, 45: 570-572, 1950.

675. Lindelius, Rolf and Salum, Inna. Alcoholism and Crime: A Com-
      parative Study of Three Groups of Alcoholics. Journal of
      Studies on Alcohol, 36(11): 1452-1457, 1978.

676. Lindelius, Rolf and Salum, Inna. Alcoholism and Criminality.
      Acta Psychiatrica Scandinavica, 49: 306-314, 1973.

677. Lindelius, Rolf and Salum, Inna. Criminality among Homeless Men.
      British Journal of Addiction, 71: 149-153, 1976.

678. Linden, L. Allvarlig komplikation vid Antabus. [Serious Compli-
      cation with Antabus.] Svenska Läkartidningen, 45: 2469-2470,
      1948.

679. Lindinger, H. Beobachtungen über den Verlauf der Alkoholkrankheit
      am Krankengut einer Heilanstalt. [Observations on the Course
      of Alcoholism in Patients in a Mental Institution.] Münchener
      Medizinische Wochenschrift, 105: 982-989, 1963.

680. Linn, Margaret W. Attrition of Older Alcoholics from Treatment.
      Addictive Diseases, 3(3): 437-447, 1978.

681. Linn, Margaret W., Linn, Bernard S. and Greenwald, Shayna R. The
      Alcoholic Patient in the Nursing Home. Aging and Human De-
      velopment, 3(3): 273-277, 1972.

682. Linsky, Arnold S. The Changing Public Views of Alcoholism.
      Quarterly Journal of Studies on Alcohol, 31(3): 692-704,
      1970.

683. Lipscomb, Wendell R. Mortality Rate among Treated Alcoholics:
      A Three-Year Follow-Up Study. Quarterly Journal of Studies
      on Alcohol, 20: 596-603, 1959.

684. Lipscomb, Wendell R. and Sulka, Elaine. Some Factors Affecting
      the Geographic Comparison of Alcoholism Prevalence Rates:
      Implications for the Use of the Jellinek Estimation Formula.
      Quarterly Journal of Studies on Alcohol, 22(4): 588-596,
      1961.

685. Liss, L. Additional Case of Marchiafava-Bignami Disease. Neur-
      ology, 28: 1069, 1978.

686. Locke, Ben Z. Outcome of First Hospitalization of Patients with
      Alcoholic Psychoses. Quarterly Journal of Studies on Alco-
      hol, 23(4): 640-643, 1962.

687. Locke, Ben Z. and Duvall, Henrietta J. Alcoholism among First
      Admissions to Ohio Public Mental Hospitals. Quarterly Jour-
      nal of Studies on Alcohol, 25: 521-534, 1964.

688. Locke, Ben Z., Kramer, Morton and Pasamanick, Benjamin. Alcoholic
      Psychoses among First Admissions to Public Mental Hospitals
      in Ohio. Quarterly Journal of Studies on Alcohol, 21: 457-
      474, 1960.

689. Lolli, Giorgio, Golder, Grace M., Serianni, Emidio, Bonfiglio, Gio-
      vanni and Balboni, Claudia. Choice of Alcoholic Beverage
      among 178 Alcoholics in Italy. Quarterly Journal of Studies
      on Alcohol, 19(2): 303-308, 1958.

690. Lolli, Giorgio, Schesler, Esther and Golder, Grace M. Choice of
      Alcoholic Beverage among 105 Alcoholics in New York. Quar-
      terly Journal of Studies on Alcohol, 21(3): 475-482, 1960.

691. Lolli, Giorgio, Serianni, Emidio, Golder, Grace M., and Luzzatto-
      Fegiz, Pierpaolo. Alcohol in Italian Culture: Food and Wine
      in Relation to Sobriety among Italians and Italian Americans.
      Monograph No. 3. Glencoe, Illinois: The Free Press; and
      New Haven, Connecticut: Publications Division, Yale Center
      of Alcohol Studies, 1958, especially pages 84, 105-112.

692. Lowe, George D., Hodges, H. Eugene and Johnson, Ann B. Deaths
      Associated with Alcohol in Georgia, 1970. Quarterly Journal
      of Studies on Alcohol, 35(1): 215-220, 1974.

693. Lowe, W.C. and Thomas, S.D. Death Expectancies in Alcoholic and
      Nonalcoholic Persons. Journal of Clinical Psychology, 33(4):
      1154-1156, 1977.

694. Lowenfels, A.B., Masih, B., Lee, T.C. and Rohman, M. Effect of
      Intravenous Alcohol on the Pancreas. Archives of Surgery,
      96: 440-441, 1967.

695. Lucas, Max. L'alcoolisme dans les hospices de vieillards de la
      région parisienne. [Alcoholism in Homes for the Aged in the
      Paris Region.] Revue de l'Alcoolisme, 15: 268-284, 1969.

696. Lucia, Salvatore P. A History of Wine and Medicine. Philadel-
      phia, Pennsylvania: J.B. Lippincott, 1963.

697. Lucia, Salvatore P. Balm for the Autumnal Years. Western Medi-
      cine, 4: 170-171, 178, 1963.

698. Ludwig, Jurgen, Garrison, Charles O. and Baggenstoss, Archie H.
      Latent Hepatic Cirrhosis: A Study of 95 Cases. American
      Journal of Digestive Diseases, N.S. 15(1): 7-14, 1970.

699. Luff, K., Heiser, H., Kunze, J. and Lutz, F.U. Die alkoholbe-
      dingte Leistungsminderung in Abhängigkeit vom Lebensalter.
      [Alcohol-Induced Performance Decrease as a Function of Age.]
      Hefte zur Unfallheilkunde, 121: 410-417, 1975.

700. Lugand, A. La situation dans un hospice de l'Isère. [The Situ-
      ation in a Home in Isère.] Revue de l'Alcoolisme, 15: 61-63,
      1969.

701. Lund, E., Geill, T., Dam, H. and Kristensen, G. Serum Lipids in
      Relation to the Intake of Alcohol and Sodium Chloride.
      Nature, 191: 1095-1097, 1961.

702. Lundin, D.V. Medication Taking Behavior of the Elderly: A Pilot
      Study. Drug Intelligence and Clinical Pharmacy, 12: 518-522,
      1978. (Also in: The PharmChem Newsletter, 8(6): 1-5, 1979.)

703. Lundquist, G.A.R. Klinisk alkoholforskning. [Clinical Alcohol
      Research.] Läkartidningen, 62: 1813-1819, 1965.

704. Lustig, B.   On Alcoholism in the Aged.   In: Scriptum Geriatricum.
        Ed. W. Doberauer.   Vienna: Gesellschaft für Geriatric, 1963,
        pages 207-211.

705. Lutterotti, A. de.   L'alcool nella vecchiaia: Aspetti clinici,
        con particulare riguardo alla miocardiopatia alcoolica.
        [Alcohol in the Elderly: Clinical Aspects, with Particular
        Regard to Alcoholic Cardiomyopathy.]   Giornale di Geronto-
        logia, 22: 1010-1013, !974.

706. Lutterotti, A. de.   L'aspect social de l'alcoolisme dans la vieil-
        lesse.   [The Social Aspect of Alcoholism in Old Age.]   Revue
        de l'Alcoolisme, 15:   49-57, 1969.   (Also in: Revue d'Hy-
        giene et de Médecine Sociale, 15(8): 751-760, 1967.)

707. Lutterotti, A. de.   Rapporti tra etilismo cronico e miocardiopatia
        nell'anziano.   [Relations between Chronic Alcoholism and
        Myocardiopathy in the Aged.]   Giornale di Gerontologia, 15:
        45-50, 1967.

708. Lutz, E.G.   Neuroleptic-Induced Parkinsonism Facilitated by Alco-
        hol.   Journal of the Medical Society of New Jersey, 75: 473-
        474, 1978.

M

709. Macaron, C., Feero, S. and Goldflies, M. Hypothermia in Wer-
       nicke's Encephalopathy. Postgraduate Medicine, 65(2): 241-
       242, 246, 1979.

710. McCarthy, F.M. and Hayden, J., Jr. Ethyl Alcohol by the Oral
       Route as a Sedative in Dentistry. Journal of the American
       Dental Association, 96: 282-287, 1978.

711. McClean, Heather E., Stewart, A.W., Riley, C.G. and Beaven, D.W.
       Vitamin C Status of Elderly Men in a Residential Home.
       New Zealand Medical Journal, 86(598): 379-382, 1977.

712. Macco, G. di. Alcoolismo e senescenza. [Alcoholism and Sen-
       escence.] Rivista di Gerontologia e Geriatria, 10(5): 217-
       221, 1961. (Also in: L'alimentazione nell'età senile.
       Ed. M. Peretz. Rome: Il Pensiero Scientifico, 1961,
       pages 347-352.)

713. McCusker, Jane, Cherubin, Charles E. and Zimberg, Sheldon. Pre-
       valence of Alcoholism in General Municipal Hospital Popula-
       tion. New York State Journal of Medicine, 71: 751-754, 1971.

714. MacDonald, Mary J. Pub Sociotherapy. The Canadian Nurse, 68:
       30-32, 1972.

715. McEntee, W.J. and Mair, R.G. Memory Impairment in Korsakoff's
       Psychosis: A Correlation with Brain Noradrenergic Activity.
       Science, 202: 905-907, 1978.

716. McGinnis, C.A. and Ryan, C.W. The Influence of Age on MMPI Scores
       of Chronic Alcoholics. Journal of Clinical Psychology, 21:
       271-272, 1965.

717. McGlone, Frank B. and Kick, Ella. Health Habits in Relation to
       Aging. Journal of the American Geriatrics Society, 26(11):
       481-488, 1978.

718. MacKay, A. and Stevenson, R.D. Gastric Ulceration Induced by
       Sprionolactone. The Lancet, 1: 481, 1977.

719. McLachlan, J.F.C. An MMPI Discriminant Function to Distinguish
     Alcoholics from Narcotics Addicts; Effects of Age, Sex, and
     Psychopathology. Journal of Clinical Psychology, 31: 163-
     165, 1975.

720. MacLennan, A. Pilot Project Helps Elderly Drinkers. The Journal,
     5(6): 2, 1976.

721. McMichael, A.J. Increases in Laryngeal Cancer in Britain and
     Australia in Relation to Alcohol and Tobacco Consumption
     Trends. The Lancet, 1(8076): 1244-1247, 1978.

722. Madeddu, A. Alcoolismo e vecchiaia: Incidenza della patrologia
     mentale--alcune considerazioni clinico-statische. [Alco-
     holism and Old Age: Incidence of Mental Pathology--Some
     Clinico-Statistical Considerations.] Giornale di Geronto-
     logia, 15(1): 51-61, 1967.

723. Magliari, G., Zara, E. and Rini, U. Considerazioni sugli aspetti
     sociali dell'alcoolismo nella populazione del Salento. [Con-
     siderations on the Social Aspects of Alcoholism in the Popu-
     lation of Salento.] Folia Psychiatrica, 4(2): 143-163, 1961.

724. Maglinte, Dean D.T., Taylor, Silvija D. and Ng, Anastacio C.
     Gastrointestinal Perforation by Chicken Bones. Radiology,
     130: 597-599, 1979.

725. Maisto, S.A., Sobell, L.C., Zelhart, P.F., Connors, G.J. and
     Cooper, T. Driving Records of Persons Convicted of Driving
     under the Influence of Alcohol. Journal of Studies on Alco-
     hol, 40: 70-77, 1979.

726. Majtényi, C. A Female Case of Marchiafava-Bignami Syndrome.
     Neuropatologia Polska, 26: 241-247, 1978.

727. Mäkelä, Klaus. Alkoholin ongelmakäyttäjät kulutustutkimuksen
     mukaan. [Excessive Drinking According to a Study on Alcohol
     Consumption.] Alkoholikysymys, 38: 160-171, 1970.

728. Mäkelä, Klaus. Ika ja alkoholinkäyttö; kulutustutkimuksen ennak-
     koraportti. [Age and Alcohol Use; Preliminary Report on a
     Consumption Study.] Alkoholipoliittisen Tutkimuslaitoksen,
     Tutkimusseloste (No. 56), Helsinki: Oy ALKO Ab, 1970.

729. Malamud, N. and Skillicorn, S.A. Relationship between the Wer-
     nicke and the Korsakoff Syndrome. American Medical Associ-
     ation Archives of Neurological Psychiatry, 76: 585-596, 1956.

730. Maliković, Božidar, Divac, Marija, Blagojević, Miodrag and Kirko-
     vić, Mara. Osobenosti grupne psihoterapije alkoholičara
     starijeg životnog doba. [Special Features of Group Psycho-
     therapy of Elderly Alcoholics.] Socijalna Psihijatrija, 4:
     67-76, 1976. (Also in: Alkoholizam, 16(1-2): 7-17, 1976.)

731. Malzberg, Benjamin. A Study of First Admissions with Alcoholic
     Psychoses in New York State, 1943-44. Quarterly Journal of
     Studies on Alcohol, 8(2): 274-295, 1947-48.

732. Malzberg, Benjamin. First Admissions with Alcoholic Psychoses in
     New York State, Year Ended March 31, 1948. Quarterly Journal
     of Studies on Alcohol, 10(3-4): 461-470, 1949.

733. Malzberg, Benjamin. The Expectation of an Alcoholic Mental Dis-
     order in New York State, 1920, 1930, and 1940. Quarterly
     Journal of Studies on Alcohol, 4(4): 523-534, 1943-44.

734. Manceaux, A.-G., Sutter, J.M., Pélicier, Y. and Escoute, R. Mal-
     adie de Launois-Bensaude éthylique. [Alcoholic Launois-Ben-
     saude Disease.] Revue d'Oto-Neuro-Ophtalmologie, 29: 377-
     379, 1957.

735. Mancinella, A., Liuti, G., Paolucci, M. and Baietti, M. Further
     Observations on Chronic Alcoholic Hepatopathy in the Aged:
     The Zieve Syndrome. Clinica Terapeutica, 87(1): 75-88, 1978.

736. Mancinella, A., Paolucci, M., Liuti, G. and Baietti, M. Le epato-
     patie alcooliche nell'anziano: Aspetti patogenetici, clinici
     e terapeutici. [Alcoholic Liver Diseases in the Aged: Patho-
     genetic, Clinical and Therapeutic Aspects.] Clinica Tera-
     peutica, 85(3): 293-309, 1978.

737. Mann, S.K. and Mann, N.S. Pancreatic Ascites. American Journal
     of Gastroenterology, 71(2): 186-192, 1979.

738. Mansfeld, E. Über das körperliche und soziale Schicksal von 100
     chronischen Vieltrinkern einer schwäbischen Kleinstadtbrau-
     erei. [On the Physical and Social Fate of 100 Chronic Heavy
     Drinkers of a Swabian Smalltown Brewery.] Zeitschrift für
     die gesamte Neurologie und Psychiatrie, 170: 344-372, 1940.

739. Marchezotti, A., Vazquez, S., Fellner, J., Burucua, J.E., Garcia-
     Fernandez, J.C., Aragon, R. and Koch, O.R. Metabolismo del
     alcohol en alcoholistas crónicos con y sin daño hepático.
     [Alcohol Metabolism in Chronic Alcoholics with and without
     Liver Damage.] Medicina, 36: 99-106, 1976.

740. Marden, Parker G. Alcohol Abuse and the Aged. Rockville, Mary-
     land: The National Institute on Alcohol Abuse and Alcohol-
     ism, 1976, pages 1-21.

741. Marfil, R.G., Luna, S., Hafiz, A. and Cohen, S. Nail-Patella Syn-
     drome. Canadian Medical Association Journal, 101: 706-709,
     1969.

742. Markiewicz, D. and Brennenstuhl, W. Zmiany neuropatologiczne w
     alkoholizmie z objawami psychodegeneracji. [Neuropathologi-
     cal Changes in Alcoholics with Psychodegenerative Symptoms.]
     Problemy Alkzmu, 17(6): 1-3, 1969.

743. Maron, Barry J. and Ferrans, Victor J. Ultrastructural Features
      of Hypertrophied Human Ventricular Myocardium. Progress in
      Cardiovascular Diseases, 21(3): 207-238, 1978.

744. Martel, F. Nouvelle approche expérimentale du traitement de
      l'alcoolisme: La régulation metabolique. [New Experimental
      Approach to the Treatment of Alcoholism: Metabolic Regula-
      tion.] Toxicomanies, 7: 233-247, 1974.

745. Martini, G.A. and Wienbeck, M. Begünstigt Alkohol die Entstehung
      eines Barrett-Syndroms: Endobrachyösophagus? [Does Alcohol
      Enhance the Development of Barrett's Syndrome: Endobrachy-
      esophagus?] Deutsche Medizinische Wochenschrift, 99: 434-
      439, 1974.

746. Massé, H. L'alcoolisme facteur de mortalité; son incidence sur
      les principales causes de décès. [Alcoholism as a Cause in
      Mortality; its Effect on the Main Causes of Death.] Nouvelle
      Presse Médicale, 1: 1857-1860, 1972.

747. Maughan, W.Z., Muller, S.A. and Perry, H.O. Porphyria Cutanea
      Tarda Associated with Lymphoma. Acta Dermato-Venereologica,
      59: 55-58, 1979.

748. Maurisset, O. and Oustry, G. Intérêt d'un nouveau traitement de
      l'éthylisme en pneumologie. [Value of a New Treament of
      Alcoholics in Pneumology.] Semaine des Hôpitaux de Paris,
      55(3-4), 165-168, 1979.

749. Maxwell, Milton A. Drinking Behavior in the State of Washington.
      Quarterly Journal of Studies on Alcohol, 13(2): 219-239,
      1952.

750. Maxwell, Milton A., Lemere, Frederick and O'Hollaren, Paul.
      Changing Characteristics of Private-Hospital Alcoholic
      Patients: A Twenty-Year Time-Trend Analysis. Quarterly
      Journal of Studies on Alcohol, 19(2): 309-315, 1958.

751. Mayfield, Demmie G. Alcohol Problems in the Aging Patient. In:
      Drug Issues in Geropsychiatry. Ed. William E. Fann and
      George L. Maddox. Baltimore: Williams and Wilkins, 1974,
      pages 35-40.

752. Meade, T.W., Chakrabarti, R., Haines, A.P., North, W.R.S. and
      Stirling, Yvonne. Characteristics Affecting Fibrinolytic
      Activity and Plasma Fibrinogen Concentrations. British Med-
      ical Journal, 1: 153-156, 1979.

753. Medhus, Asbjörn. Alcohol Problems among Male Disability Pension-
      ers. Scandinavian Journal of Social Medicine, 4(3): 145-149,
      1976.

754. Medhus, Asbjörn and Hansson, Holger. Alcohol Problems among
      Female Gonorrhoea Patients. Scandinavian Journal of Social
      Medicine, 4(3): 141-143, 1976.

755. Meer, Bernard and Amon, Albert H.   Age-Sex Preference Patterns of
      Alcoholics and Normals.   Quarterly Journal of Studies on Al-
      cohol, 24(3): 417-431, 1963.

756. Menier, [H.], Payan, and Touzet, [P.].   La fréquence de l'alcool-
      isme et son retentissement sur la capacité de travail chez
      les salariés du bâtiment et des trauvaux publics, âgés de
      60 ans et plus.   [The Incidence of Alcoholism and Its Effect
      on the Working Capacity of Wage Earners Aged 60 and Over in
      Construction and Public Works.]   Revue de l'Alcoolisme, 16:
      304-313, 1970.

757. Mercês-de-Mello, M.L. and Castelão, M.O.   Quelques réflexions au
      sujet de l'alcoolisme au 3e âge.   [Some Thoughts on Alcohol-
      ism among Senior Citizens.]   (Abstract.)   In: Papers Pre-
      sented at the 24th International Institute on the Prevention
      and Treatment of Alcoholism.   Ed. E.J. Tongue.   Lausanne:
      International Council on Alcohol and Addictions, 1978,
      page 453.

758. Mercuri, Gabriele.   Chronic Alcoholism and Schizophrenia: Des-
      cription of Two Cases.   Lavoro Neuropsichiatrico, 57(1-2):
      291-297, 1975.

759. Mercuri, Gabriele.   Gelosia morbosa e criminalità; descrizione di
      un caso.   [Morbid Jealousy and Crime; Description of One
      Case.]   Lavoro Neuropsichiatrico, 57(3): 171-182, 1975.

760. Messert, Bernard, Orrison, William W., Hawkins, Michael J. and
      Quaglieri, Charles E.   Central Pontine Myelinolysis: Con-
      siderations on Etiology, Diagnosis, and Treatment.   Neurology,
      29(2): 147-160, 1979.

761. Messiha, F.S., Croy, D.J., Hartman, R.J. and Geller, I.   Critical
      Variables Involved in Behavioral and Biochemical Actions of
      Ethanol.   Proceedings of the Western Pharmacology Society,
      17: 200-203, 1974.

762. Meyer, M., Wechsler, S., Shibolet, S., Jedwab, M., Harell, A., and
      Edelstein, S.   Malabsorption of Vitamin D in Man and Rat with
      Liver Cirrhosis.   Journal of Molecular Medicine, 3: 29-38,
      1978.

763. Meyer, N.G.   Diagnostic Distribution of Admissions to Inpatient
      Services of State and County Mental Hospitals, United States,
      1975.   Mental Health Statistical Note, 138, 1-16, 1977.

764. Mezey, E. and Holt, P.R.   Loss of the Characteristic Features of
      Atypical Human Liver Alcohol Dehydrogenase during Purifica-
      tion.   Life Sciences, 8: 245-251, 1969.

765. Mezzena, R.   L'emodinamica nell'etilista anziano con partiocolare
      riguardo al circolo periferico.   [Hemodynamics in the Aged
      Alcoholic with Special Reference to Peripheral Circulation.]
      Giornale di Gerontologia, 15: 107-114, 1967.

766. Michaux, L., Gallot, H.-M. and Dubois, J.-C. Accès dipsomaniaques avec délire épisodique de possession chez un éthylique chronique. [Attacks of Dipsomania with Episodic Delirium of Possession in a Chronic Alcoholic.] Annales Médico-Psychologiques, 105: 385-390, 1947.

767. Michelis, M.F., Mitchell, B. and Davis, B.B. "Bicarbonate Resistant" Metabolic Acidosis in Association with Ethylene Glycol Intoxication. Clinical Toxicology, 9: 53-60, 1976.

768. Michigan. Office of Services to the Aging. Seniors and Substance Abuse Task Force. Substance Abuse among Michigan's Senior Citizens: Current Issues and Future Directions. Lansing, Michigan, August 1978, pages 1-41.

769. Miles, C. Toward a Classification of Drinking Behavior. M.A. Thesis. Rutgers University, 1969.

770. Miller, P. Treatment of Alcoholics in Nursing Homes. Paper presented at the 1976 National Alcoholism Forum: National Council on Alcoholism, May 6-13, Washington, D.C.

771. Mills, P.N., McSween, R.N.M. and Watkinson, G. Cholestasis in Acute Alcoholic Liver Disease. The Lancet, 1(8060): 388, 1978.

772. Minirth, F. The Effects of Religious Backgrounds on Emotional Problems. Journal of the Arkansas Medical Society, 72: 227-234, 1975.

773. Mishara, Brian L. and Kastenbaum, Robert. Alcohol and Old Age. New York: Grune and Stratton, 1980.

774. Mishara, Brian L. and Kastenbaum, Robert. Wine in the Treatment of Long-Term Geriatric Patients in Mental Institutions. Journal of the American Geriatrics Society, 22(2): 88-94, 1974.

775. Mishara, Brian L., Kastenbaum, Robert, Baker, Frank and Patterson, Robert D. Alcohol Effects in Old Age: An Experimental Intigation. Social Science and Medicine, 9(10): 535-547, 1975.

776. Misra, P.C. Nitrazepam (Mogadon) Dependence. British Journal of Psychiatry, 126: 81-82, 1975.

777. Misuse of Drugs and Alcohol by the Elderly Reported Rising. Behavior Today, 7(24): 3-4, 1976.

778. Miyazaki, M. Circulatory Effect of Ethanol, with Special Reference to Cerebral Circulation. Japanese Circle Journal, 38: 381-385, 1974.

779. Modini, R.A., Molina, J.C. and Saforcada, E. Alcoholismo en un
     grupo laboral ferroviario. [Alcoholism in a Group of Rail-
     road Workers.] Acta Psiquiatrica y Psicologica de América
     Latina, 23: 50-57, 1977.

780. Mogar, R.E., Wilson, W.M. and Helm, S.T. Personality Subtypes of
     Male and Female Alcoholic Patients. International Journal of
     Addiction, 5: 99-113, 1970.

781. Molinier, A., Bovagnet, G. and Tchourumoff, N. Les manifestations
     cardiovasculaires au cours des epreuves de conditionnement
     dans la desintoxication éthylique. [Cardiovascular Signs in
     the Course of Conditioning Tests in Alcohol Detoxication.]
     Semaine des Hôpitaux de Paris, 42: 1562-1568, 1966.

782. Moll, J.M. "Amnestic" or "Korsakoff's" Syndrome with Alcoholic
     Aetiology: An Analysis of Thirty Cases. Journal of Mental
     Science, 61: 424-443, 1915.

783. Monckton-Copeman, P.W., Cripps, D.J., and Summerly, R. Cutaneous
     Hepatic Porphyria and Oestrogens. British Medical Journal,
     1: 461-463, 1966.

784. Monti, M. Microcalorimetric Measurements of Heat Production in
     Erythrocytes of Patients with Liver Diseases. Scandinavian
     Journal of Haematology, 19(3): 313-318, 1977.

785. Moon, Louis E. and Patton, Robert E. The Alcoholic Psychotic in
     the New York State Mental Hospitals, 1951-1960. Quarterly
     Journal of Studies on Alcohol, 24(4): 664-681, 1963.

786. Moorhead, Harry H. Study of Alcoholism with Onset Forty-Five
     Years or Older. Bulletin of the New York Academy of Medicine,
     34(2): 99-108, 1958.

787. Morino, G. Studio Statistico-Clinico sui ricvoerati per alcoolis-
     mo nel decennio 1954-1963 nell'Ospedale Psichiatrico Provin-
     ciale di Cuneo. [Statistical-Clinical Study of Patients Ad-
     mitted for Alcoholis during the 1954-1963 Decade to the Psy-
     chiatric Hospital of the Province of Cuneo.] Minerva Medica,
     58: 565-570, 1967.

788. Morowtiz, H.J. The Wine of Life. Hospital Practice, 13(3): 173,
     176, 1978.

789. Morrison, S.A., Russell, R.M., Carney, E.A. and Oaks, E.V. Zinc
     Deficiency: A Cause of Abnormal Dark Adaptation in Cirrho-
     tics. American Journal of Clinical Nutrition, 31(2): 276-
     281, 1978.

790. Mortality from Alcoholism. Statistical Bulletin of the Metropoli-
     tan Life Insurance Company, 58: 2-5, 1977.

791. Moss, M.C. L'épidémiologie de l'alcoolisme dans un comté anglais.
     [Epidemiology of Alcoholism in an English County.] Toxico-
     manies, 3: 175-191, 1970.

792. Mukerjee, Chitta M. Reactivation of Pulmonary Tuberculosis in New South Wales, 1975. Medical Journal of Australia, 2: 333-335, 1978.

793. Mulford, Harold A. Drinking and Deviant Drinking, U.S.A., 1963. Quarterly Journal of Studies on Alcohol, 25: 634-650, 1964.

794. Mulford, Harold A. and Miller, Donald E. Drinking in Iowa. I. Sociocultural Distribution of Drinkers. Quarterly Journal of Studies on Alcohol, 20: 704-726, 1959.

795. Mulford, Harold A. and Miller, Donald E. Drinking in Iowa. II. The Extent of Drinking and Selected Sociocultural Categories. Quarterly Journal of Studies on Alcohol, 21: 26-39, 1960.

796. Mulford, Harold A. and Miller, Donald E. Drinking in Iowa. V. Drinking and Alcoholic Drinking. Quarterly Journal of Studies on Alcohol, 21(3): 483-499, 1960.

797. Mulford, Harold A. and Miller, Donald E. Measuring Public Acceptance of the Alcoholic as a Sick Person. Quarterly Journal of Studies on Alcohol, 25(2): 314-323, 1964.

798. Mulford, Harold A. and Miller, Donald E. The Prevalence and Extent of Drinking in Iowa, 1961: A Replication and an Evaluation of Methods. Quarterly Journal of Studies on Alcohol, 24(1): 39-53, 1963.

799. Muller, Christian. Spezielle Alterspsychiatrie. [Special Geriatric Psychiatry.] In: Alterspsychiatrie. [Geriatric Psychiatry.] Stuttgart: Georg Thieme, 1967, pages 108-164.

800. Müller-Limmroth, W. and Schneble, H. Neue Erkenntnisse zur Leistungsfähigkeit des Kraftfahrers, zu ihren Grenzen und zu ihrer Verminderung durch Medikamente und Alkohol. [New Facts Regarding Drivers' Performance; Limits and Deterioration in Driving Performance Caused by Medicines and Alcohol.] Blutalkohol, 15: 226-240, 1978.

801. Municchi, L. Studio statistico-clinico sulle psicosi alcooliche osservate nell'ospedale psichiatrico di Alessandria nel periodo 1954-1965. [A Statistical-Clinical Study of Alcoholic Psychoses Observed at the Psychiatric Hospital of Alessandria in the Period 1954-1965.] Rassegna di Studi Psichiatrici, 56: 433-456, 1967.

802. Murdock, Harold R., Jr. The Effect of Table Wines on Blood Glucose Levels in the Geriatric Subject. Geriatrics, 27(7): 93-96, 1972.

803. Murphy, George E. Suicide and Attempted Suicide. Hospital Practice, 12(11): 73-81, 1977.

804. Murphy, George E., Armstrong, John W., Jr., Hermele, Stephen L.,
        Fischer, John R. and Clendenin, William W. Suicide and Al-
        coholism: Interpersonal Loss Confirmed as a Predictor. Ar-
        chives of General Psychiatry, 36(1): 65-69, 1979.

805. Murphy, M., Warnes, H. and Moore, P. Serum Magnesium, Hepatic
        Enzymes and Chronic Alcoholism. Psychiatric Journal of the
        University of Ottawa, 3(1): 15-19, 1978.

806. Myerson, David J. Alcoholic Person Grows Older. Journal of Geri-
        atric Psychiatry, 11(2): 175-190, 1978.

807. Myerson, David J. Organic Problems in the Aged: Brain Syndromes
        and Alcoholism--As the Alcoholic Person Grows Older. Journal
        of Geriatric Psychiatry, 11(2): 175-189, 1978.

808. Myrhed, M. and Floderus, B. Alcohol Consumption in Relation to
        Factors Associated with Ischemic Heart Disease: A Cotwin
        Control Study. Acta Geneticae Medicae et Gemellologiae,
        25: 129-132, 1976.

N

809. Nashold, R.D. and Wadsack, H. Alcoholism in Wisconsin, 1959-1961. *Wisconsin Medical Journal*, 62: 249-251, 1963.

810. National Council on the Aging, Inc. Research and Evaluation Department. The Effects of Retirement on Drinking Behavior. Prepared for the National Institute on Alcohol Abuse and Alcoholism. (Report No. PB 281-143.) Springfield, Virginia: U.S. National Technical Information Service, 1977.

811. Nelson, Leonard. Alcoholism in Zuni New Mexico. *Preventive Medicine*, 6(1): 152-166, 1977.

812. Neundörfer, B. and Gössinger, S. Klinische Diagnose und Verlauf der Wernicke-Encephalopathie. [Clinical Diagnosis and Course of Wernicke's Encephalopathy.] *Der Nervenarzt*, 48(9): 500-504, 1977.

813. Newman, S.E. The EEG Manifestations of Chronic Ethanol Abuse: Relation to Cerebral Cortical Atrophy. *Annals of Neurology*, 3(4): 299-304, 1978.

814. Nicholls, Peter, Edwards, Griffith and Kyle, Elspeth. Alcoholics Admitted to Four Hospitals in England. II. General and Cause-Specific Mortality. *Quarterly Journal of Studies on Alcohol*, 35(3): 841-855, 1974.

815. Nicolas, G., Bouhour, J.B., Gaillard, A. and Horeau, J. Le coeur dans la cirrhose alcoolique; à propos de 200 cas cliniques et 72 cas anatomo-cliniques. [The Heart in Alcoholic Cirrhosis; Concerning 200 Clinical Cases and 72 Anatomico-clinical Cases.] *Revue de l'Alcoolisme*, 16: 267-273, 1970.

816. Nicolas, G., Gaillard, A., Bouhour, J.B. and Horeau, J. L'athérosclérose coronarienne chez les cirrhotiques; étude anatomique de 50 cas. [Coronary Atherosclerosis in Cirrhotics; Anatomical Study of 50 Cases.] *Revue de l'Alcoolisme*, 16: 274-280, 1970.

817. Nielsen, J.M. and Courville, C.B. Central Necrosis of the Corpus Callosum (Marchiafava-Bignami's Disease). Bulletin of the Los Angeles Neurological Society, 8: 81-88, 1943.

818. Nilsson, B.E. and Westlin, N.E. Changes in Bone Mass in Alcoholics. Clinical Orthopaedics and Related Research, 90: 229-232, 1973.

819. Nilsson, L.H. and Hultman, E. A Comparison of the Bromsulphthalein and Galactose Elimination Test in Patients with Either Chronic Bowel Inflammation or Alcoholic Liver Disease. Scandinavian Journal of Gastroenterology, 9: 319-323, 1974.

820. Nizzoli, V. and Solimè, F. Fosfolipidi per via endovenosa in terapia neuropsichiatrica. [Intravenous Phospholipids in Neuropsychiatric Therapy.] Minerva Medica, 57: 913-917, 1966.

821. Nolan, Anthony J. and Peretz, Dwight I. Beer as an Adjunct to the Low Sodium Diet. British Columbia Medical Journal, 15(10): 300-302, 1973.

822. Nussenfeld, Sidney R., Davis, Joseph H., Nagel, Eugene L. and Hirschman, Jim C. Alcohol Benefit for the Geriatric Patient. Journal of the American Medical Association, 227(4): 439-440, 1974.

823. Nuttall, R.L. and Costa, P.T. Drinking Patterns as Affected by Age and by Personality Type. Gerontologist, 15(5): 35, 1975.

824. Nyfors, A. Liver Biopsies from Psoriatics Related to Methotrexate Therapy. 3. Findings in Post-Methotrexate Liver Biopsies from 160 Psoriatics. Acta Pathologica Microbiologica Scandinavica, 85(4): 511-518, 1977.

825. Nyfors, A. and Poulsen, H. Liver Biopsies from Psoriatics Related to Methotrexate Therapy. 2. Findings Before and After Methotrexate Therapy in 88 Patients; a Blind Study. Acta Pathologica Microbiologica Scandinavica, 84A: 262-270, 1976.

826. O'Brien, M.J., Kennedy, J.D. and Little, M.P.G. Alcohol-Related
     Deaths in the West of Ireland. Irish Journal of Medical
     Science, 144: 292-303, 1975.

827. Offerhaus, L. De gevaren van het gebruik van geneesmiddelen bij
     bejaarden--implicaties van de veranderde farmacokinetiek en
     farmacodynamiek voor een juiste indicatiestelling en dos-
     ering. [The Dangers of Drug Use in the Aged--Implications
     of Changed Pharmacokinetics and Pharmacodynamics for Correct
     Indications and Dosage.] Nederlands Tijdschrift voor Genees-
     kunde, 121(42): 1660-1161, 1977.

828. Ojeda, V.J. Metastatic Oat Cell Carcinoma Simulating Liver Cir-
     rhosis. New Zealand Medical Journal, 86: 480-481, 1977.

829. Okada, Hiroshi, Horibe, Hiroshi, Ohno, Yoshiyuki, Hayakawa, Nori-
     hiko and Aoki, Nobuo. A Prospective Study of Cerebrovascular
     Disease in Japanese Rural Communities, Akabane and Asahi.
     Part I: Evaluation of Risk Factors in the Occurrence of
     Cerebral Hemorrhage and Thrombosis. Stroke, 7(6): 599-607,
     1976.

830. Okamura, K. A Study on Mallory Bodies: Isolation, Ultrastruc-
     ture and Preliminary Biochemical Characterization of Mallory
     Bodies from Livers of Alcoholic Cirrhosis and Malignant
     Hepatoma. Acta Pathologica Japonica, 26(6): 649-670, 1976.

831. O'Keane, M., Russell, R.I. and Goldberg, A. Ascorbic Acid
     Status of Alcoholics. Journal of Alcoholism, 7: 6-11, 1972.

832. Older Problem Drinkers: Their Special Needs, and a Nursing Home
     Geared to Those Needs. Alcohol Health and Research World
     (Spring Experimental Issue), pages 12-17, 1975.

833. Oldershausen, H.-F. von. Über die Pathogenese alkoholischer
     Leberschäden. [On the Pathogenesis of Alcoholic Liver
     Damage.] Deutsche Medizinische Wochenschrift, 89: 867-874,
     1964.

834. O'Leary, M.R., Radford, L.M., Chaney, E.F. and Schau, E.J. As-
      sessment of Cognitive Recovery in Alcoholics by Use of the
      Trail-Making Test. Journal of Clinical Psychology, 33: 579-
      582, 1977.

835. O'Neill, S. The Nurse and the Elderly Patient. In: New Thoughts
      on Old Age. Ed. Robert Kastenbaum. New York: Springer
      Publishing Co., 1964, pages 186-190.

836. Orford, J., Hawker, A. and Nicholls, P. An Investigation of an
      Alcoholism Rehabilitation Halfway House. I. Types of Client
      and Modes of Discharge. British Journal of Addiction, 69:
      213-224, 1974.

837. Orloff, M.J., Duguay, L.R. and Kosta, L.D. Criteria for Selection
      of Patients for Emergency Portacaval Shunt. American Journal
      of Surgery, 134(1): 146-152, 1977.

838. Ornstein, Peter. The Alcadd Test as a Predictor of Post-Hospital
      Drinking Behavior. Psychological Reports, 43: 611-617, 1978.

839. Oscar-Berman, M., Sahakian, B.J. and Wikmark, G. Spatial Proba-
      bility Learning by Alcoholic Korsakoff Patients. Journal of
      Experimental Psychology: Learning and Memory, 2: 215-222,
      1976.

840. Outreach Is Key in Program for Older Drinkers. NIAAA Information
      and Feature Service, page 1, 1976.

841. Ovenstone, I.M.K. and Kreitman, N. Two Syndromes of Suicide.
      British Journal of Psychiatry, 124: 336-345, 1974.

842. Overall, J.E., Hoffmann, N.G. and Levin, H. Effects of Aging,
      Organicity, Alcoholism, and Functional Psychopathology on
      WAIS Subtest Profiles. Journal of Consulting and Clinical
      Psychology, 46(6): 1315-1322, 1978.

843. Owens, J.M., Quinn, J.T. and Graham, J. Drinking Patterns in an
      Irish County. Part 2. Irish Medical Journal, 70: 550-555,
      1977.

P

844. Pach, J., Marek, Z., Bogusz, M. and Stasko, W. The Clinical Appearance and Blood Alcohol Level in Acute Poisoning and Blood Alcohol Level in Fatal Non-Treated Poisoning. Acta Pharmacologica et Toxicologica, 41(2): 362-368, 1977.

845. Palutke, W.A., Boyd, C.B. and Carter, G.R. Pasturella multocida Septicemia in a Patient with Cirrhosis; Report of a Case. American Journal of Medical Science, 266: 305-308, 1973.

846. Pape, H.-D., Hausamen, J.E. and Neumann, D. Stomatologische Erhebungen bei 1970 Altersheim- und Trinkerheilanstaltinsassen. [Stomatological Findings in 1970 Inmates of Old Age Homes and Alcoholic Rehabilitation Institutions.] Deutsche Zahnärztliche Zeitschrift, 25: 103-105, 1970.

847. Paradoxical Refuge. (Editorial.) New England Journal of Medicine, 245: 268-269, 1951.

848. Parisella, Rosemary M. and Pritham, Gordon H. Effect of Age on Alcohol Preference by Rats. Quarterly Journal of Studies on Alcohol, 25(2): 248-252, 1964.

849. Parker, Elizabeth S. and Noble, Ernest P. Alcohol and the Aging Process in Social Drinkers. Journal of Studies on Alcohol, 41(1): 170-178, 1980.

850. Parl, Fritz E., Lev, Robert, Thomas, Eapen and Pitchumoni, Capecomorin S. Histologic and Morphometric Study of Chronic Gastritis in Alcoholic Patients. Human Pathology, 10(1): 45-56, 1979.

851. Pascarelli, Emil F. Alcoholism and Drug Addiction in the Elderly: Old Drug Addicts Do Not Die, Nor Do They Just Fade Away. Geriatric Focus, 11(5): 1, 4-5, 1972.

852. Pascarelli, Emil F. An Update on Drug Dependence in the Elderly. Journal of Drug Issues, 9(1): 47-54, 1979.

853. Pascarelli, Emil F. Drug Dependence: An Age-Old Problem Com-
       pounded by Old Age. Geriatrics, 29(12): 109-110, 114-115,
       1974.

854. Pascarelli, Emil F. and Fischer, William. Drug Dependence in the
       Elderly. International Journal of Aging and Human Develop-
       ment, 5(4): 347-356, 1974.

855. Pasquariello, G., Quadri, A. and Tenconi, L.T. Tryptophan→Nico-
       tinic Acid Metabolism in Chronic Alcoholics. Acta Vitamino-
       logica, 18: 3-6, 1964.

856. Patients Drink Beer in Hospital Pub. Journal of the American
       Medical Association, 212(11): 1801, 1804, 1970.

857. Patterson, Robert D., Abrahams, Ruby and Baker, Frank. Preventing
       Self-Destructive Behavior. Geriatrics, 29: 115-118, 121,
       1974.

858. Pauchant, M. and Bernard, J.M. Étude clinique d'un nouveau
       psychotrope anxiolytique: Le Ro-05-4556; à propos de 30
       cas. [Clinical Study of a New Anxiolytic Psychotropic
       Drug, Ro-05-4556; 30 Cases.] Lille Médicale, 15: 153-159,
       1970.

859. Pearl, Raymond. Alcohol and Longevity. New York: Alfred A. Knopf
       Publishing Co., 1926.

860. Pearl, Raymond. Alcohol and Mortality. Plymouth, Massachusetts:
       Mayflower Press, 1922.

861. Peck, David G. Alcohol Abuse and the Elderly: Social Control
       and Conformity. Journal of Drug Issues, 9(1): 63-71, 1979.

862. Pedrazzoli, M., Tafner, G. and Bajocchi, E. L'alcoolismo nel
       Trentino; rilievi clinico-statistici su 822 pazienti maschi
       ricoverati nel 1971 presso una Divisione di Medicina Gener-
       ale. [Alcoholism in Trento; Clinico-Statistical Data in a
       Series of 822 Male Patients Admitted to a General Medical
       Division during 1971.] Minerva Medica, 65: 778-789, 1974.

863. Pelka-Slugocki, M.D. and Slugocki, L. Alcoholism and Female
       Crime in Poland. International Journal of Offender Therapy,
       21: 174-183, 1977.

864. Pell, Sidney and D'Alonzo, C.A. A Five-Year Mortality Study of
       Alcoholics. Journal of Occupational Medicine, 15(2): 120-
       125, 1973.

865. Pell, Sidney and D'Alonzo, C.A. The Prevalence of Chronic Disease
       among Problem Drinkers. Archives of Environmental Health,
       16: 679-684, 1968.

866. Pelletier, Julien. Problemes liés à la consommation excessive
     d'alcool chez les personnes âgées. [Problems Related to Ex-
     cessive Alcohol Consumption by the Aged.] Toxicomanies,
     9(2): 121-143, 1976.

867. Peppers, Larry G. and Stover, Ronald G. The Elderly Abuser: A
     Challenge for the Future. Journal of Drug Issues, 9(1): 73-
     83, 1979.

868. Péquignot, G., Chabert, C., Eydoux, H. and Courcoul, M.-A.
     Augmentation du risque de cirrhose en fonction de la ration
     d'alcool. [Increase in the Risk of Cirrhosis as a Function
     of Alcohol Intake.] Revue de l'Alcoolisme, 20: 191-202,
     1974.

869. Péquignot, Henri, Guerre, J., Christoforov, B., Laffitte-Catta,
     M., Delignieres, S. and Cassaigne, J.Y. La ponction-biopsie
     du foie dans un service de médecine interne. [Needle Biopsy
     of the Liver in an Internal Medicine Department.] Semaine
     des Hôpitaux de Paris, 54(43-44): 1319-1323, 1978.

870. Péquignot, Henri, Voisin, P., Guerre, J., Christoforov, B. and
     Portos, J.-L. Aspects de l'alcoolisme du sujet âgé hospi-
     talisé dans un service de medecine générale. [Aspects of
     Alcoholism in an Aged Patient, Hospitalized on a General
     Medical Ward.] Revue de l'Alcoolisme, 15: 33-45, 1969.

871. Pereiras, R., Jr., Chiprut, R.O., Greenwald, R.A. and Schiff, E.R.
     Percutaneous Transhepatic Cholangiography with the "Skinny"
     Needle: A Rapid, Simple, and Accurate Method in the Diagno-
     sis of Cholestasis. Annals of Internal Medicine, 86(5): 562-
     568, 1977.

872. Perkins, Clifton T. Proposals for the Establishment of Institu-
     tions for the Care and Treatment of Inebriates in Massachu-
     setts and Connecticut. Quarterly Journal of Studies on Alco-
     hol, 4(1): 93-109, 1943-44.

873. Peron, N. and Gayno, M. Atrophie cérébrale des éthyliques. [Cere-
     bral Atrophy in Alcoholics.] Revue Neurologique, 94: 621-624,
     1956.

874. Pessayre, D., Lebrec, D., Descatoire, V., Peignoux, M. and Ben-
     hamou, J.-P. Mechanism for Reduced Drug Clearance in Patients
     with Cirrhosis. Gastroenterology, 74: 566-571, 1978.

875. Peters, G.A., Jr. Emotional and Intellectual Concomitants of Ad-
     vanced Chronic Alcoholism. Journal of Consulting and Clin-
     ical Psychology, 20: 390, 1956.

876. Peters, U.H. and Gille, G. Über die körperlichen Gründe körper-
     lich begründbarer Psychosen. [On the Somatic Causes of So-
     matically Based Psychoses.] Deutsche Medizinische Wochen-
     schrift, 98: 967-970, 1973.

877. Petersen, David M. Introduction: Drug Use among the Elderly.
      Addictive Diseases, 3(3): 305-309, 1978.

878. Petersen, David M. and Thomas, Charles W. Acute Drug Reactions
      among the Elderly. Journal of Gerontology, 30(5): 552-556,
      1975.

879. Petersen, David M. and Whittington, Frank J. Drug Use Among the
      Elderly: A Review. Journal of Psychedelic Drugs, 9(1):
      25-37, 1977.

880. Petersen, David M., Whittington, Frank J. and Payne, Barbara P.,
      eds. Drugs and the Elderly: Social and Pharmacological
      Issues. Springfield, Illinois: Charles C. Thomas, 1979.

881. Peterson, L.M. and Brooks, J.R. Lethal Pancreatitis: A Diagnos-
      tic Dilemma. American Journal of Surgery, 137(4): 491-496,
      1979.

882. Petrilowitsch, Nikolaus. Die Problemkreise alternder Mensches im
      Lichte der suizidalen Kranken. [Problem Areas in Older Per-
      sons as Reflected in Suicidal Patients.] In: Probleme der
      Psychotherapy alternder Menschen. [Problems of Psychotherapy
      among Older Persons.] 2nd ed. New York: Karger, 1968.

883. Pfister, A.K., McKenzie, J.V., Dinsmore, H.P. and Edman, C.D.
      Extracorporeal Dialysis for Methanol Intoxication. Journal
      of the American Medical Association, 197: 1041-1043, 1966.

884. Philippe, J.M., Dusehu, E. and Fievet, P. Rupture de varices du
      ligament colo-pariétal; cause possible d'hémopéritoine chez
      le cirrhotique. [Variceal Rupture of the Coloparietal Liga-
      ment; a Possible Cause of Hemoperitoneum in Cirrhotic Pa-
      tients.] Nouvelle Presse Médicale, 8: 659, 1977.

885. Phillips, Lorne A. An Application of Anomy Theory to the Study of
      Alcoholism. Journal of Studies on Alcohol, 37(1): 78-84,
      1976.

886. Pindborg, J.J. Oral Cancer and Precancer as Diseases of the Aged.
      Community Dentistry and Oral Epidemiology, 6: 300-307, 1978.

887. Pintar, K., Wolanskyj, B.M. and Gubbay, E.R. Alcoholic Cardio-
      myopathy. Canadian Medical Association Journal, 93: 103-107,
      1965.

888. Pisani, V.D., Jacobson, G.R. and Berenbaum, H.L. Field Dependence
      and Organic Brain Deficit in Chronic Alcoholics. Internation-
      al Journal of the Addictions, 8(3): 559-564, 1973.

889. Pitchumoni, Capecomorin S. and Glass, G.B.J. Patterns of Gastri-
      tis in Alcoholics. Biological Gastroenterology, 9(1): 11-16,
      1976.

890. Pitchumoni, Capecomorin S., Lopes, J.D. and Glass, G.B.J. The
     Prevalence of Gastric Autoantibodies in Chronic Alcoholics.
     American Journal of Gastroenterology, 64: 187-190, 1975.

891. Plutchik, Robert and DiScipio, William J. Personality Patterns in
     Chronic Alcoholism (Korsakoff's Syndrome), Chronic Schizo-
     phrenia, and Geriatric Patients with Chronic Brain Syndrome.
     Journal of the American Geriatrics Society, 22(11): 514-516,
     1974.

892. Plutchik, Robert, McCarthy, Martin and Hall, Bernard H. Changes
     in Elderly Welfare Hotel Residents during a One-Year Period.
     Journal of the American Geriatrics Society, 23(6): 265-270,
     1975.

893. Plutchik, Robert, McCarthy, Martin, Hall, Bernard H., and
     Silverberg, Shirley. Evaluation of a Comprehensive Psy-
     chiatric and Health Care Program for Elderly Welfare Tenants
     in a Single-Room Occupancy Hotel. Journal of the American
     Geriatrics Society, 21: 452-459, 1973.

894. Poikolainen, K. Alcohol Poisoning Mortality in Four Nordic Coun-
     tries. (Alcohol Research in the Northern Countries, Finnish
     Foundation for Alcohol Studies, Vol. 28.) Helsinki; The
     Foundation [Distributed by Rutgers University Center of Alco-
     hol Studies], 1977.

895. Poikolainen, K. Dödligheten i alkoholförgiftning i Danmark, Fin-
     land, Norge och Sverige. [Mortality in Alcoholic Intoxication
     in Denmark, Finland, Norway and Sweden.] Nordic Medicine,
     94(3): 90-92, 1979.

896. Poikolainen, K. Finska alkoholseder och mortaliteten. [Drinking
     Patterns in Finland and Mortality.] Alkoholpolitik, 41: 70-
     77, 1978. (Also as: Suomalaiset juomatavat ja kuolleisuus.
     [Finnish Drinking Patterns and Mortality.] Alkoholipoliti-
     ikka, 43: 100-106, 1978.

897. Poliquin, N. and Straker, M. A Clinical Psychogeriatric Unit:
     Organization and Function. Journal of the American Geri-
     trics Society, 25: 132-137, 1977.

898. Pollak, S. Der alkoholisierte Fussgänger als Opfer tödlicher
     Strassenverkehrunfälle. [The Alcoholized Pedestrian as Vic-
     tim of Fatal Traffic Accidents.] Wiener Klinische Wochen-
     schrift, 88: 206-209, 1976.

899. Popa, G., Niculescu, M., Iordăcheanu, L. and Hurjui, V. Troubles
     hématologiques dans l'alcoolisme aigu. [Hematologic Findings
     in Alcoholics Following Intoxication.] Folia Haematologica,
     105: 71-78, 1978.

900. Popp, L. Statistischer Beitrag zur Frage der Aetiologie der Leber-cirrhose. [Statistical Contribution to the Problem of the Etiology of Liver Cirrhosis.] Zeitschrift für Klinische Medizin, 142: 106-141, 1943.

901. Poppe, W. and Hentschel, F. Alkoholismus bei Bürgern im höheren Lebensalter. Eigenarten des Alkoholismus beim alten Menschen. [Alcoholism among Senior Citizens. Peculiarities of Old-Age Alcoholism.] Deutsche Gesundheitswesen, 33: 56-59, 1978.

902. Poppe, W. and Hentschel, F. Eigenarten des Alkoholismus bei alten Menschen. [Peculiarities of Alcoholism in Old Persons.] Paper presented at the 23rd International Institute in the Prevention and Treatment of Alcoholism. Dresden: ICAA Publication, 1977, pages 238-239.

903. Post, Felix. Management of Senile Psychiatric Disorders. British Medical Journal, 5631: 627-630, 1968.

904. Potential for Alcoholism Greater among Elderly. NIAAA Information and Feature Service (from the National Clearinghouse for Alcohol Information of the National Institute on Alcohol Abuse and Alcoholism), No. 62: 6, 1979.

905. Powell, C. The Use and Abuse of Drugs in Brain Failure. Age and Ageing (Supplement), 6: 83-90, 1970.

906. Powell, L.W., Mortimer, R. and Harris, O.D. Cirrhosis of the Liver: A Comparative Study of the Four Major Aetiological Groups. Medical Journal of Australia, 58: 941-950, 1971.

907. Praag, H.M. van. Psychotropic Drugs in the Aged. Comprehensive Psychiatry, 18(5): 429-442, 1977.

908. Preimate, E. Ya, Mitrofanov, M.P. and Anspoka, Ya I. Korrelyat-sionnyi analiz klinicheskikh i morfologicheskikh dannykh, poluchennykh pri epidemiologicheskom izuchenii ishemicheskoi bolezni serdtsa. [Correlative Analysis of Clinical and Morphological Data Obtained from an Epidemiological Study of Ischemic Heart Disease.] Latvijas PSR Zinotnu Akademijas Vestis, 3: 90-96, 1972.

909. Priest, R.G. The Homeless Person and the Psychiatric Services: An Edinburgh Survey. British Journal of Psychiatry, 128: 128-136, 1976.

910. Prince, Joyce. Drinking Habits of Women in Holloway Prison and Those Dealt with at a London Court. In: Proceedings of an International Symposium on The Drunkenness Offence held from 15 to 17 May, 1968, at the Institute of Psychiatry, Maudsley Hospital, London, S.E.5. under the Auspices of Camberwell Council on Alcoholism and International Council on Alcohol and Addictions. Oxford: Pergamon Press, 1969, pages 27-33, especially pages 29-30, 32-33.

911. Probst, J.   Die Bedeutung des durch Entzug provozierten Delirium
      tremens in der gesetzlichen Unfallversicherung. [The Legal
      Significance of Delirium Tremens Provoked by Abstinence in
      Accident Insurance.] Monatsschrift für Unfallheilkunde, 71:
      313-318, 1968.

912. Program Fosters Recovery of Alcoholic Pilots. NIAAA Information
      and Feature Service, page 1, 1976.

913. Prost, G., Dechavanne, Martin C., Evreux, M. and Tolot, F. Survie
      des cirrhoses éthyliques decompensées. [Survival Rate in
      Decompensated Alcoholic Cirrhosis.] Nouvelle Presse Médicale,
      1: 3031-3033, 1972.

914. Prys-Williams, G. and Glatt, Max M. The Incidence of (Long-
      Standing) Alcoholism in England and Wales. British Journal
      of Addiction, 61: 257-268, 1966.

915. Püschel, K., Kleiber, M. and Brinkmann, B. Blutalkoholkonzen-
      tration von 0.62% überlebt. [Survival with a Blood Alcohol
      Concentration of 0.62%.] Blutalkohol, 16: 217-220, 1979.

916. Putkonen, T. Pellagra alkoholistilla. [Pellagra in an Alcoholic.]
      Duodecim, 68: 204-208, 1952.

Q

917. Quirk, D.A. Public policy Notes. 1. Landmark Pension Reform Is Law. 2. Alcoholism--Recent Developments in Legislation and Research. Industrial Gerontology, 1(4): 62-67, 1974.

R

918. Rada, R.T., Porch, B.E., Dillingham, C., Kellner, R. and Porec, J.B. Alcoholism and Language Function. Alcoholism: Clinical and Experimental Research, 1(3): 199-205, 1977.

919. Rahmani, R., Dan, M., Fishel, B., Yedvab, M. and Shibolet, S. Fatal Encephalopathy Due to Chronic Lead Poisoning. Harefuah, 93: 246-249, 1977.

920. Rathbone-McCuan, Eloise. Social Variables of Geriatric Alcoholism. Presented at the National Council on Alcoholism Forum, Washington, D.C., May 1976.

921. Rathbone-McCuan, Eloise and Bland, John. A Treatment Typology for the Elderly Alcohol Abuser. Journal of the American Geriatrics Society, 23(12): 553-557, 1975.

922. Rathbone-McCuan, Eloise and Bland, John. Diagnostic and Referral Considerations for the Geriatric Alcoholic and Aging Problem Drinker. Presented at the Gerontological Society's 27th Annual Meeting, Portland, Oregon, October 28-November 1, 1974.

923. Rathbone-McCuan, Eloise, Lohn, Harold, Levenson, Julia and Hsu, James. Community Survey of Aged Alcoholics and Problem Drinkers. Report prepared under Grant No. 1R18-AA01734-01 for the National Institute on Alcohol Abuse and Alcoholism, June 1976. Baltimore, Maryland: Levindale Geriatric Research Center, 1976. Distributed by NTIS, Springfield, Virginia, 1976.

924. Rathbone-McCuan, Eloise and Triegaardt, Jean. The Older Alcoholic and the Family. Alcohol Health and Research World, 3(4): 7-12, 1979.

925. Ravina, A. L'alcoolisme chez les sujets âgés: Colloque annuel du groupement medical d'études sur l'alcoolisme. [Alcoholism in the Aged: Annual Colloquium of the Medical Group for Studies on Alcoholism.] Nouvelle Presse Médicale, 77(12): 445, 1969.

926. Rehfeld, J.F., Juhl, E. and Hilden, M. Carbohydrate Metabolism
      in Alcohol-Induced Fatty Liver; Evidence for an Abnormal
      Insulin Response to Glycagon in Alcoholic Liver Disease.
      Gastroenterology, 64: 445-451, 1973.

927. Reisner, H. Das chronische subdurale Hämatom--Pachymeningeosis
      haemorrhagica interna. [Chronic Subdural Haematoma and
      P.H.I.] Der Nervenarzt, 50(2): 74-78, 1979.

928. Reynolds, Ingrid, Harnas, June, Gallagher, Hugh and Bryden, David.
      Drinking and Drug Taking Patterns of 8,516 Adults in Sydney.
      Medical Journal of Australia, 2(21): 782-785, 1976.

929. Riccitelli, M.L. Alcoholism in the Aged--Modern Concepts. Jour-
      nal of the American Geriatrics Society, 15(2): 142-147, 1967.

930. Richer, G., Houle, G., Morcos, N., Montambault, J., Turgeon, F.
      and Marleau, D. Rôle du virus de l'hépatite B dans la
      genèse de la maladie hépatique alcoolique. [Role of the
      Hepatitis B Virus in the Origin of Alcoholic Liver Disease.]
      Union Médicale du Canada, 103: 1027-1032, 1974.

931. Riding, J. Wet Beriberi in an Alcoholic. British Medical Jour-
      nal, 3: 79, 1975.

932. Riege, W.H. Inconstant Nonverbal Recognition Memory in Korsakoff
      Patients and Controls. Neuropsychologia, 15: 269-276, 1977.

933. Riesner, K. and Janssen, W. Alcohol-Induced Cardiomyopathy and
      Sudden Heart Death. Beiträge zur Gerichtlichen Medizin, 36:
      351-358, 1978.

934. Riley, John W., Marden, Charles F. and Lifshitz, Marcia. The
      Motivational Pattern of Drinking: Based on the Verbal Re-
      sponses of a Cross-Section Sample of Users of Alcoholic
      Beverages. Quarterly Journal of Studies on Alcohol, 9(3):
      353-362, 1948-49.

935. Ringel, E. and Schinko, H. Eine weibliche Alkoholhysterie. [Al-
      coholic Hysteria in a Woman.] Wiener Zeitschrift für Nerven-
      heilkunde und ihren Grenzgebiete, 12: 154-164, 1955.

936. Roberts, Kathleen E. Intravenous Therapy in Geriatric Patients.
      In: Clinical Principles and Drugs in the Elderly. Ed. Jos-
      eph T. Freeman. Springfield, Illinois: Charles C. Thomas,
      1963, pages 339-358.

937. Roch, M. L'alcoolisme et son rôle en pathologie interne. [Alco-
      holism and Its Role in Internal Pathology.] Basle: Ben-
      no Schwabe and Company, 1940.

938. Rodrigo, R. and Egana, E. Alcohol: NAD Oxidoreductase in Brain
      of Rats from a Colony Fed Dilute Ethanol for Many Gener-
      ations. Journal of Neurochemistry, 25: 645-647, 1975.

939. Roebuck, Julian B. and Kessler, Raymond G. The Etiology of Alco-
        holism: Constitutional, Psychological, and Sociological Ap-
        proaches. Springfield, Illinois: Charles C. Thomas, 1972,
        especially pages 155, 212-214.

940. Rojas-MacKenzie, R. and De-Los-Ríos-Osorio, J. Habitos de inges-
        tion de bebidas alcohólicas en una comunidad rural de An-
        tioquia, Columbia. [Drinking Habits in a Rural Community of
        Antioquia, Colombia.] Boletin da la Oficina Sanitaria Pan-
        Americana, 83: 148-162, 1977.

941. Rooke, M.L., and Wingrove, C.R. Gerontology: An Annotated Bib-
        liography. Washington, D.C.: University Press of America,
        1977.

942. Room, Robin. Drinking Patterns in Large U.S. Cities: A Compari-
        son of San Francisco and National Samples. Quarterly Jour-
        nal of Studies on Alcohol, Supplement No. 6: 28-57, 1972.

943. Rose, C.L. and Cohen, M.L. Relative Importance of Physical
        Activity for Longevity. Annals of the New York Academy of
        Sciences, 301: 671-702, 1977.

944. Rosen, H.M., Yoshimura, N., Hodgman, J.M. and Fischer, J.E. Plas-
        ma Amino Acid Patterns in Hepatic Encephalopathy of Differing
        Etiology. Gastroenterology, 72, 483-487, 1977.

945. Rosen, Yale and Won, Ok Hee. Phlegmonous Enterocolitis. American
        Journal of Digestive Diseases, 23(3): 248-256, 1978.

946. Rosenberg, Nathan, Laessig, Ronald H. and Rawlings, Robert R. Al-
        cohol, Age and Fatal Traffic Accidents. Quarterly Journal of
        Studies on Alcohol, 35(2): 473-489, 1974.

947. Rosenblatt, Sidney M., Gross, Milton M. and Chartoff, Susan. Mar-
        ital Status and Multiple Psychiatric Admissions for Alco-
        holism. Quarterly Journal of Studies on Alcohol, 30(2):
        445-447, 1969.

948. Rosenblatt, Sidney M., Gross, Milton M., Malenowski, Beverly,
        Broman, Melinda and Lewis, Eastlyn. Marital Status and
        Multiple Psychiatric Admissions for Alcoholism; a Cross-
        Validation. Quarterly Journal of Studies on Alcohol, 32(4):
        1092-1096, 1971.

949. Rosin, Arnold J. and Glatt, Max M. Alcohol Excess in the Elderly.
        Quarterly Journal of Studies on Alcohol, 32: 53-59, 1971.

950. Ross, O. and Kreitman, N. A Further Investigation of Differences
        in the Suicide Rates of England and Wales and of Scotland.
        British Journal of Psychiatry, 127: 575-582, 1975.

951. Roth, Barbara and Williams, Erma Polly. Drinking and Alcohol Prob-
        lems among the Aged: A Survey of Findings with Bibliography,
        Preliminary Report, Introduction. New Brunswick, New Jersey:
        Center of Alcohol Studies, Rutgers University, 1972.

952. Roth, Barbara and Williams, Erma Polly. Alcoholism and Problem
      Drinking among Older Persons; Drinking and Alcohol Problems
      among the Aged: A Survey of Findings with Bibliography.
      Center of Alcohol Studies, Rutgers University, 1973. [See
      Entry #182.]

953. Roth, W. "The Drunken Silen" with Symptoms of Liver Insuf-
      ficiency. Hautarzt, 30(1): 25-26, 1979.

954. Rotter, H. Der Änderung der Toleranz bei chronischen Alkoholikern.
      [Change of Tolerance in Chronic Alcoholics.] Wiener Medi-
      zinische Wochenschrift, 109: 388-390, 1959.

955. Roussel, A., Gignoux, M., Verwaerde, J.C., Segol, P., Abbatucci,
      J.S. and Valla, A. Esophageal Cancer in Western France:
      Retrospective Analysis of 1400 Cases. Bulletin of Cancer,
      64(1): 61-66, 1977.

956. Rowe, John W., Wands, Jack R., Mezey, Esteban, Waterbury, Larry A.,
      Wright, John R., Tobin, Jordan and Andres, Reubin. Familial
      Hemochromatosis: Characteristics of the Precirrhotic Stage
      in a Large Kindred. Medicine, 56(3): 197-211, 1977.

957. Rubenstein, A.E. and Wainapel, S.F. Acute Hypokalemic Myopathy
      in Alcoholism: A Clinical Entity. Archives of Neurology,
      34: 553-555, 1977.

958. Rubino, G.F., Capellaro, F., Pettinati, L. and Scansetti, G. Il
      tasso alcoolemico nei guidatori di automezzi in rapporto agli
      incidenti stradali. [Blood Alcohol Level in Chauffeurs in
      Relation to Road Accidents.] Minerva Medica, 51: 555-558,
      1960.

959. Rueff, B., Prandi, D., Degos, F., Sicot, J., Degos, J.-D., Sic-
      ot, C., Maillard, J.-N., Fauvert, R. and Benhamou, J.-P.
      A Controlled Study of Therapeutic Portacaval Shunt in Alco-
      hol Cirrhosis. The Lancet, 1: 655-659, 1976.

960. Rushing, William A. Alcoholism and Suicide Rates by Status Set
      and Occupation. Quarterly Journal of Studies on Alcohol,
      29(2): 399-412, 1968.

961. Rushing, William A. Suicide and the Interaction of Alcoholism
      (Liver Cirrhosis) with the Social Situation. Quarterly Jour-
      nal of Studies on Alcohol, 30(1): 93-103, 1969.

962. Ryan, C. and Butters, Nelson. Accelerated Aging in Chronic Alco-
      holics: Evidence from Tests of Learning and Memory. Alco-
      holism: Clinical and Experimental Research, 3(2): 193, 1979.

S

963. Sadoun, Roland, Lolli, Giorgio, and Silverman, Milton. Drinking
in French Culture. Monograph No. 5. New Brunswick, New Jersey: Publications Division, Rutgers Center of Alcohol
Studies, 1965.

964. Sainsbury, P. Suicide in the Middle and Later Years. In: Medical and Clinical Aspects of Aging. Ed. H. Blumenthal.
New York: Columbia University Press, 1962, pages 97-102.

965. Saint Leger, A.S., Cochrane, A.L. and Moore, F. Factors Associated with Cardiac Mortality in Developed Countries with
Particular Reference to the Consumption of Wine. The Lancet,
1: 1017-1020, 1979.

966. Salter, William T. Use of Drugs for Older People. Geriatrics,
7: 317-323, 1952.

967. Salum, I., ed. Delirum Tremens and Certain Other Acute Sequels
of Alcohol Abuse: A Comparative Clinical, Social, and Prognostic Study. Acta Psychiatrica Scandinavica (Supplement
No. 235): 1-145, 1972.

968. Salzman, Leon. The Problem of Alcohol and the Aging Crisis.
In: Drug Abuse: Modern Trends, Issues, and Perspectives.
Proceedings of the Second National Drug Abuse Conference,
New Orleans, Louisiana, 1975. Ed. Arnold Schecter, Har-
old Alksne, and Edward Kaufman. New York and Basle: Mar-
cel Dekker, 1978, pages 939-945.

969. Samorajski, Thaddeus, Rolsten, C. and Pratte, K.A. Dihydroergo-
toxine (Hydergine[R]) and Ethanol-Induced Aging of C57BL/6J
Male Mice. Pharmacology, 16 (Supplement 1): 36-44, 1978.

970. Samorajski, Thaddeus, Strong, John R. and Sun, Albert Y. Dihydro-
ergotoxine (Hydergine) and Alcohol-Induced Variations in
Young and Old Mice. Journal of Gerontology, 32 (2): 145-152,
1977.

971. Samorajski, Thaddeus, Strong, John R., Sun, G.Y., Sun, Albert Y.
      and Seamen, R. Dihydroergotoxine and Ethanol: Physiologi-
      cal and Neurochemical Variables in Male Mice. Gerontology
      (Supplement), 24(1): 43-54, 1978.

972. Saphir, W. and Spurlock, J. Alcoholic Neuropathy and Laennec's
      Cirrhosis. Illinois Medical Journal, 97: 278-280, 1950.

973. Sarg, M.J., Jr. and Pitchumoni, Capecomorin S. Case Report:
      Hypophosphatemic Hemolytic Syndrome of Alcoholics--A Common
      City Hospital Problem. American Journal of Medical Science,
      276: 231-235, 1978.

974. Sarley, V.C. and Stepto, R.C. Use of Wine in Extended Care
      Facilities. In: Wine and Health. Ed. Salvatore P. Lucia.
      San Francisco: Fortune House, 1969; Menlo Park, California:
      Pacific Coast Publishers, 1969, pages 28-30.

975. Sarley, V.C. and Tyndall, F.W. Wine Is Beneficial to Geriatric
      Nonpatients, Too. Nursing Homes, 20: 27-30, 1971.

976. Satinder, K. Paul. Interactions of Age, Sex and Long-Term Alcohol
      Intake in Selectively Bred Strains of Rats. Journal of
      Studies on Alcohol, 36(11): 1493-1507, 1975.

977. Satterwhite, T.K., Kageler, W.V., Conklin, R.H., Portnoy, B.L.
      DuPont, H.L. Disseminated Sporotrichosis. Journal of the
      American Medical Association, 240: 771-772, 1978.

978. Sattler, Jerome M. and Pflugrath, Joan Frissell. Future-Time
      Perspective in Alcoholics and Normals. Quarterly Journal
      of Studies on Alcohol, 31(2): 839-850, 1970.

979. Saturnus, K.-S. Tödliche Unfälle von Fussgängern im Strassenver-
      kehr. [Fatal Pedestrian Accidents in Street Traffic.] Zeit-
      schrift für Rechtsmedizin, 73: 279-289, 1973.

980. Saunders, Sarah J. A Search for a Means of Reducing Problem
      Drinking, and Aiding the Problem Drinkers, in a Senior Citi-
      zens Home (Lambert Lodge--City of Toronto, Progress Report at
      the End of One Year). Substudy No. 638. Toronto, Ontario:
      Addiction Research Foundation, 1974.

981. Saunders, Sarah J. Reducing Problem Drinking in a Home for the
      Aged: Castleview Wychwood Towers. Substudy No. 745. Toron-
      to, Ontario: Addiction Research Foundation, 1976.

982. Saunders, Sarah J. Second Annual Report: Reducing Problem
      Drinking in a Home for the Aged. Substudy No. 745. Toron-
      to, Ontario: Addiction Research Foundation, 1976, pages 1-
      6.

983. Saunders, W.M. and Kershaw, P.W. The Prevalence of Problem
      Drinking and Alcoholism in the West of Scotland. British
      Journal of Psychiatry, 133: 493-499, 1978.

984. Savage, R.D., Gaber, L.B., Button, P.G., Bolton, N. and Cooper, A.
      Personality and Adjustment in the Aged. New York: Academic
      Press, 1977.

985. Saville, P.D. Changes in Bone Mass with Age and Alcoholism.
      Journal of Bone and Joint Surgery, 47: 492-499, 1965.

986. Sawka, Edward. Alcohol Use among Edmonton Elderly: A Pilot Sur-
      vey, Final Report. Edmonton: Alberta Alcoholism and Drug
      Abuse Commission, 1978.

987. Scarda, G. and Parziale, G. Gli ematomi sub-durali cronici: Con-
      siderazioni su 85 Casi. [Chronic Subdural Hematoma: 85
      Cases.] Lavoro Neuropsichiatrico, 62(1-2): 125-132, 1978.

988. Schenkenberg, Thomas, Dustman, R.E. and Beck, E.C. Cortical
      Evoked Responses of Hospitalized Geriatrics in Three Diag-
      nostic Categories. Proceedings of the American Psychologi-
      cal Association, 80: 671-672, 1972.

989. Schimpff, R.M., Lebrec, D., Dannadieu, M. and Repellin, A.M.
      Serum Somatomedin Activity Measured as Sulphation Factor in
      Peripheral, Hepatic and Renal Veins of Patients with Alco-
      holic Cirrhosis. Acta Endocrinologica, 88(4): 729-736,
      1978.

990. Schlossberg, D. Septicemia Caused by DF-2. Journal of Clinical
      Microbiology, 9: 297-298, 1979.

991. Schmalbruch, H. and Dume, T. Klinische inapperente Alkoholschädi-
      gung der menschlichen Herzmuskelzelle. [Clinically Inap-
      parent Damage to the Human Myocardial Cell Caused by Alco-
      hol.] Archiv für Kreislaufforschung, 58: 202-227, 1969.

992. Schmid, Calvin F. Mortality from Alcoholism in the United States.
      Quarterly Journal of Studies on Alcohol, 1(3): 432-441, 1940.

993. Schmidt, Wolfgang and de Lint, Jan. Causes of Death of Alcoholics.
      Quarterly Journal of Studies on Alcohol, 33(1): 171-185, 1972.

994. Schmidt, Wolfgang and de Lint, Jan. Mortality Experiences of Male
      and Female Alcoholic Patients. Quarterly Journal of Studies
      on Alcohol, 30(1): 112-118, 1969.

995. Schoenen, J. and Delwaide, P.J. Indications des bêta-bloqueurs
      en neurologie. [Use of Beta-Blocking Agents in Clinical
      Neurology.] Acta Clinica Belgica, 33(2): 130-140, 1978.

996. Schottenfeld, D., Gantt, R.C., and Wynder, E.L. The Role of Al-
      cohol and Tobacco in Multiple Primary Cancers of the Upper
      Digestive System, Larynx and Lung: A Prospective Study.
      Preventive Medicine, 3: 277-293, 1974.

997. Schuckit, Marc A. An Overview of Alcohol and Drug Abuse Problems
      in the Elderly, page 127. [See Entry #1114.]

998. Schuckit, Marc A. Geriatric Alcoholism and Drug Abuse. Geronto-
      logist, 17(2): 168-174, 1977.

999. Schuckit, Marc A. The High Rate of Psychiatric Disorders in Elder-
      ly Cardiac Patients. Angiology, 28(4): 235-247, 1977.

1000. Schuckit, Marc A. and Miller, Patricia L. Alcoholism in Elderly
      Men: A Survey of a General Medical Ward. Annals of the
      New York Academy of Sciences, 273(8): 558-571, 1976.

1001. Schuckit, Marc A., Miller, Patricia L. and Hahlbohm, Dewey. Un-
      recognized Psychiatric Illness in Elderly Medical-Surgical
      Patients. Journal of Gerontology, 30(6): 655-660, 1975.

1002. Schuckit, Marc A., Morrissey, Elizabeth R. and O'Leary, Michael R.
      Alcohol Problems in Elderly Men and Women. Addictive Dis-
      eases, 3(3): 405-416, 1978.

1003. Schuckit, Marc A. and Pastor, Paul A., Jr. The Elderly as a Unique
      Population: Alcoholism. Alcoholism, 2(1): 31-38, 1978.

1004. Schuckit, Marc A., Rimmer, J., Reich, and Winokur, G. Alcoholism:
      Antisocial Traits in Male Alcoholics. British Journal of
      Psychiatry, 117(54): 575-576, 1970.

1005. Schuster, R. The Involvement of Retired Persons in Alcohol-
      Induced Offenses in Middle Hessen. Beiträge zur Gericht-
      lichen Medizin, 36: 269-274, 1978.

1006. Schwartz, Arthur N., ed. Psychosocial Adjustment to Aging:
      A Selected Bibliography. Alcoholism. Alcoholism: Clinical
      and Experimental Research, 2(1): 31-38, 1978.

1007. Scott, Doreen C. and Parker, John H. On to the Pub, or Is It
      Worth It? Nursing Homes, 24(4): 12-14, 1975.

1008. Scully, R.E., Galdabini, J.J. and McNeely, B.U. Fever, Confusion
      and Gastrointestinal Symptoms in a 64-Year-Old Man. (Case
      Records of the Massachusetts General Hospital.) New England
      Journal of Medicine, 300: 243-252, 1979.

1009. Second Special Report on Alcohol and Health. Lifelines, 17(2):
      13-16, 1975.

1010. Segal, B.M. The Effect of the Age Factor on Alcoholism. In:
      Currents of Alcoholism. Vol. 2. Ed. Frank A. Seixas.
      New York: Grune and Stratton, 1977, pages 377-393.

1011. Seixas, Frank A. Alcoholism in the Elderly: Introduction. Al-
      coholism: Clinical and Experimental Research, 2: 15, 1978.

1012. Seliger, R.V. Alcoholism in the Older Age Groups. Geriatrics,
      3: 166-170, 1948.

1013.   Seltzer, Benjamin and Benson, D.F.   The Temporal Pattern of Retro-
        grade Amnesia in Korsakoff's Disease.   Neurology, 24: 527-
        530, 1974.

1014.   Seltzer, Benjamin and Sherwin, Ira.   "Organic Brain Syndromes":
        An Empirical Study and Critical Review.   American Journal of
        Psychiatry, 135(1): 13-21, 1978.

1015.   Seltzer, M.L., Gikas, P.W. and Huelke, D.F., eds.   Prevention of
        Highway Injury.   (Proceedings of Symposium, April 1967, Spon-
        sored by the University of Michigan School of Medicine and
        Highway Safety Research Institute.)   Ann Arbor, Michigan:
        Highway Safety Research Institute, 1969.

1016.   Sereny, G., Mehta, B. and Sethna, D.   Chronic Alcoholic Cardio-
        myopathy: Fact or Fiction.   Drug and Alcohol Dependence,
        3(5): 331-343, 1978.

1017.   Serra, C. and Zanetti, G.   La mortalità nel delirium tremens.
        [Mortality in Delirium Tremens.]   Archivio per la Scienze
        Mediche, 93: 84-107, 1952.

1018.   Shanta, I.I.   Povtorni spontannyi vnutribryushinnyi razryv moche-
        vogo puzyrya na fone alkogol'nogo op'yaneniya.   [Repeated
        Spontaneous Intraperitoneal Rupture of the Urinary Bladder
        Associated with Alcohol Misuse.]   Klinicheskaya Khirurgiya,
        5: 61-62, 1976.

1019.   Shephard, R.J.   Physical Activity and Aging.   London: Croom Helm
        Pub., 1978.

1020.   Siakotos, A.N. and Armstrong, D.   Age Pigment, a Biochemical In-
        dicator of Intracellular Aging.   In: Neurobiology of Aging:
        An Interdisciplinary Life-Span Approach.   Ed. J.M. Ordy and
        K.R. Brizzee.   New York and London: Plenum Press, 1975,
        pages 369-399, especially page 370.

1021.   Siakotos, A.N., Armstrong, D., Koppang, N. and Muller, J.   Bio-
        chemical Significance of Age Pigment in Neurones.   In: The
        Aging Brain and Senile Dementia.   Ed. Kalidas Nandy and
        Ira Sherwin.   New York and London: Plenum Press, 1976,
        pages 99-118, especially page 100.

1022.   Sibert, J.R.   Hereditary Pancreatitis in England and Wales.
        Journal of Medical Genetics, 15: 189-201, 1978.

1023.   Sidhu, S. and Noori, D.S.   Alcoholism and Psychotic Patients.
        American Journal of Hospital Pharmacy, 35: 654, 1978.

1024.   Silverman, E.M. and Silverman, A.G.   Granulocyte Adherence in the
        Elderly.   American Journal of Clinical Pathology, 67: 49-52,
        1977.

1025. Silverman, E.M. and Wozniak, K.J. Granulocyte Adherence in
       Chronic Alcoholics. Paper presented at the 31st Annual
       Scientific Meeting of the Gerontology Society, Dallas,
       Texas, 16-20 November, 1978.

1026. Simberkoff, M.S., Moldover, N.H. and Weiss, G. Bactericidal and
       Opsonic Activity of Cirrhotic Ascites and Nonascitic Peri-
       toneal Fluid. Journal of Laboratory and Clinical Medicine,
       91: 831-839, 1978.

1027. Simon, Alexander and Epstein, Leon J. Alternatives to Mental Hos-
       pital Care for the Geriatric Patient. Current Psychiatric
       Therapies, 10: 225-231, 1970.

1028. Simon, Alexander and Epstein, Leon J. Geropsychiatry: Behavioral
       Aspects. In: Survey Report on the Aging Nervous System.
       Ed. Gabe J. Maletta. U.S. Department of Health, Education,
       and Welfare. DHEW Publication No. (NIH) 74-296, pages 215-225.

1029. Simon, Alexander, Epstein, Leon J. and Reynolds, Lynn. Alcoholism
       among the Geriatric Mentally Ill. Proceedings of the Twen-
       tieth Annual Meeting of the Gerontological Society, page 23,
       1967.

1030. Simon, Alexander, Epstein, Leon J. and Reynolds, Lynn. Alcoholism
       in the Geriatric Mentally Ill. Geriatrics, 23(10): 125-131,
       1968.

1031. Simon, M., Bourel, M., Genetet, B., Fauchet, R., Edan, G., and
       Brissot, P. Idiopathic Hemochromatosis and Iron Overload in
       Alcoholic Liver Disease: Differentiation by HLA Phenotype.
       Gastroenterology, 73(4), Part 1: 655-658, 1977.

1032. Sinclair, J.D. The Alcohol-Deprivation Effect; Influence of
       Various Factors. Quarterly Journal of Studies on Alcohol,
       33(3): 769-782, 1972.

1033. Singh, B., Knezek, L. and Matthews, T. Characteristics and Treat-
       ment Outcomes of Older Patients in Drug Treatment Programs.
       Paper presented at 31st Annual Scientific Meeting of the
       Gerontology Society, 16-20 November, 1978, Dallas, Texas.

1034. Sîrbu, A., Stroila, N., Argintaru, D. and Berecz, L. Les résul-
       tats obtenus avec R-1625 (haloperidol) dans le traitement
       des psychoses alcooliques aiguës et subaiguës. [Results
       Obtained with R-1625 (Haloperidol) in the Treatment of Acute
       and Subacute Alcoholic Psychoses.] Alcoholism, 5: 51-53,
       1969.

1035. Smart, R.G. Spontaneous Recovery in Alcoholics: A Review and
       Analysis of the Available Research. Drug and Alcohol Depen-
       dence, 1(4): 277-285, 1976.

1036. Smart, R.G., Gray, G., Finley, J. and Carpen, R. A Comparison of
      Recidivism Rates for Alcoholic Detox Residents Referred to
      Hospitals, Halfway Houses, and Outpatient Facilities. Amer-
      ican Journal of Drug and Alcohol Abuse, 4(2): 223-232, 1977.

1037. Smith, Elliott Dunlap. Handbook of Aging: For Those Growing Old
      and Those Concerned with Them. New York: Barnes and Noble,
      1972.

1038. Smith, H.H., Jr. and Smith, L.S. WAIS Functioning of Cirrhotic
      and Non-Cirrhotic Alcoholics. Journal of Clinical Psycho-
      logy, 33(1): 309-313, 1977.

1039. Smith, James W., Johnson, L.C. and Burdick, J. Ian. Sleep, Psy-
      chological and Clinical Changes during Alcohol Withdrawal in
      NAD-Treated Alcoholics. Quarterly Journal of Studies on Al-
      cohol, 32(4): 982-994, 1971.

1040. Smith, M.A.E. and Sclare, A.B. Alcoholism in Glasgow. Scottish
      Medical Journal, 9: 514-520, 1964.

1041. Smith-Moorhouse, P.M. and Lynn, L. Analysis of the Work of an
      Alcoholic Outpatient Clinic. Practitioner, 202: 410-412,
      1969.

1042. Snyder, Veronica. Aging, Alcoholism, and Reactions to Loss.
      Social Work, 22(3): 232-233, 1977.

1043. Sobel, Bernard S. Geriatric Alcoholism and Medication Abuse:
      The Insidious Disease in America. Paper presented at the
      Annual Conference of the National Alcoholism Forum, Washing-
      ton, D.C., April 27, 1979.

1044. Solmi, G., Battisti, C. de and Zani, G. Significato dell'alcool-
      deidrogenasi epatica nell'alcoolismo cronico. [Significance
      of Hepatic Alcohol Dehydrogenase in Chronic Alcoholism.]
      Minerva Medica, 60: 4555-4561, 1969.

1045. Sorenson, K. and Fagan, F. Who's on Skid Row; the Hospitalized
      Skid Row Alcoholic. Nursing Forum, 2: 86-112, 1963.

1046. Sorenson, K. and Nielsen, J. Twenty Psychotic Males with Kline-
      felter's Syndrome. Acta Psychiatrica Scandinavica, 56(4):
      249-255, 1977.

1047. Spain, D.M. Portal Cirrhosis of the Liver: A Review of Two Hun-
      dred Fifty Necropsies with Reference to Sex Differences.
      American Journal of Clinical Pathology, 15: 215-218, 1945.

1048. Sparacio, R.R., Anziska, B. and Schutta, H.S. Hypernatremia and
      Chorea: A Report of Two Cases. Neurology, 26: 46-50, 1976.

1049. Speizer, F.E., Trey, C. and Parker, P. The Uses of Multiple
       Causes of Death Data to Clarify Changing Patterns of Cir-
       rhosis Mortality in Massachusetts. American Journal of
       Public Health, 67(4): 333-338, 1977.

1050. Spencer, H., Baladad, J., and Lewin, I. The Skeletal System.
       In: Ed. Isadore Rossman. Clinical Geriatrics. Philadel-
       phia: J.B. Lippincott Company, 1971, pages 285-300.

1051. Spern, R.A., Morrow, W.R. and Peterson, D.B. Follow-up of Schizo-
       phrenic, Geriatric, and Alcoholic First Admissions: Fulton
       1956-1959 Cohorts. Archives of General Psychiatry, 12: 427,
       1965.

1052. Spicer, F. La capacité de travail des alcooliques. [The Working
       Capacity of Alcoholics.] Alcoholism, 5: 39-42, 1969.

1053. Sprott, Richard L. and Symons, James P. Alcohol Preference in
       Young and Old Inbred Mice. Unpublished research from the
       Jackson Laboratory, Bar Harbor, Maine, supported by NIH Re-
       search Grant HD-05523 from the National Institute of Child
       Health and Human Development, [1977].

1054. Srećković, Miodrag, Grbeša, Branislav, Miljković, Srbobran and
       Vidojković, Predrag. Alcoholism in the Aged. Quarterly
       Journal of Studies on Alcohol, 33(3): 898-899, 1972.

1055. Stason, W.B., Neff, R.K., Miettinen, O.S. and Jick, H. Alcohol
       Consumption and Nonfatal Myocardial Infarction. American
       Journal of Epidemiology, 104(6): 603-608, 1976.

1056. Stathers, G.M. The Synergistic Effect of Ethanol and Chlorodyne
       in Producing Hepatotoxicity. Medical Journal of Australia,
       57: 1134-1136, 1970.

1057. Steeb, U., Richard, J., Tissot, R. and Ajuriaguerra, J. de.
       A propos des relations de la mémoire et de l'intelligence
       dans le syndrome de Korsakoff. [On the Relation of Memory
       and Intelligence in Korsakoff's Syndrome.] Annales Medico-
       Psychologiques, 127: 15-56, 1969.

1058. Stefenelli, N. and Ronge, H. Änderung der Verformbarkeit und des
       viskosimetrischen Verhaltens von Erythrozyten unter Äthanol-
       einwirkung. [The Effect of Alcohol on the Deformability and
       Rheological Properties of Erythrocytes.] Wiener Klinische
       Wochenschrift, 90: 806-808, 1978.

1059. Steinmann, B. Über Hundertjährige. [On Centenarians.] Geronto-
       logia Clinica, 8: 23-35, 1966.

1060. Stenback, Asser, Kumpulainen, Maarit and Vauhkonen, Maija-Liisa.
       Illness and Health Behavior in Septuagenarians. Journal of
       Gerontology, 33(1): 57-61, 1978.

1061. Stendig-Lindberg, G., Bergstrom, J. and Hultman, E. Hypomag-
       nesemia and Muscle Electrolytes and Metabolites. Acta
       Medica Scandinavica, 201(4): 273-280, 1977.

1062. Stieglitz, E.J. Nutrition Problems of Geriatric Medicine. Jour-
       nal of the American Medical Association, 142: 1070-1077,
       1950.

1063. Stotsky, B.A. Psychoactive Drugs for Geriatric Patients with
       Psychiatric Disorders. In: Genesis and Treatment of Psy-
       chologic Disorders in the Elderly. Ed. S. Gershon and
       A. Raskin. New York: Raven Press, 1975, pages 229-258.

1064. Straus, Robert. Alcohol and the Homeless Man. Quarterly Journal
       of Studies on Alcohol, 7(3): 360-404, 1946-1947.

1065. Straus, Robert. Escape from Custody: A Study of Alcoholism and
       Institutional Dependency as Reflected in the Life Record of
       a Homeless Man. New York: Harper and Row, 1974.

1066. Straus, Robert. The Life Record of an Alcoholic. Quarterly Jour-
       nal of Studies on Alcohol, 34: 1212-1219, 1973.

1067. Straus, Robert and Bacon, Selden D. Alcoholism and Social Sta-
       bility: A Study of Occupational Integration in 2,023 Male
       Clinic Patients. Quarterly Journal of Studies on Alcohol,
       12(2): 231-260, 1951.

1068. Strole, W.E., Jr. and Vickery, A.L., Jr. Pancreatitis with Nodu-
       lar Cutaneous Lesions and Arthritis. (Case Records of the
       Massachusetts General Hospital.) New England Journal of
       Medicine, 293: 764-769, 1975.

1069. Studies Show Seriousness of Alcoholism among the Elderly.
       The Journal, 3(2): 2, 1974.

1070. Su, C.K. and Patek, A.J., Jr. Dupuytren's Contracture; Its As-
       sociation with Alcoholism and Cirrhosis. Archives of Inter-
       nal Medicine, 126: 278-281, 1970.

1071. Subby, Peg. A Community Based Program for the Chemically Depen-
       dent Elderly. Paper Presented at the North American Congress
       on Alcohol and Drug Problems. December 1975, San Francisco,
       California; and at the 26th Annual Meeting of the ADPA,
       Chicago, Illinois, 14-18 September, 1975.

1072. Sudre, Y., Talin-D'Eyzac, A. and Becq-Giraudon, B. Le syndrome de
       Zieve; a propos de deux cas. [Zieve's Syndrome; Concerning
       Two Cases.] Semaine des Hôpitaux de Paris, 49: 849-858, 1973.

1073. Sun, Albert Y., Ordy, J. Mark and Samorajski, Thaddeus. Effects
       of Alcohol on Aging in the Nervous System. In: Neuro-
       biology of Aging: An Interdisciplinary Life-Span Approach.
       Ed. J. Mark Ordy and K.R. Brizzee. New York and London:
       Plenum Press, 1975, pages 505-520.

1074. Sun, Albert Y. and Samorajski, Thaddeus. The Effects of Age and
      Alcohol on $(Na^+ + K^{++})$-ATPase Activity of Whole Homogenate and
      Synaptosomes Prepared from Mouse and Human Brain. Journal of
      Neurochemistry, 24: 161-164, 1975.

1075. Sundby, Per. Alcoholism and Mortality. (National Institute for
      Alcohol Research, Publication No. 6.) Oslo, Norway: Uni-
      versitetsforlaget, 1967. (Distributed by Publications Div-
      ision, Rutgers Center of Alcohol Studies, New Brunswick,
      New Jersey.)

1076. Sunter, J.P., Heath, A.B. and Ranasinghe, H. Alcohol Associated
      Mortality in Newcastle upon Tyne. Medicine, Science, and
      the Law, 18: 84-89, 1978.

1077. Swenson, R. and Rater, D.A. Electrolyte Disturbances in Beer
      Drinkers. The Lancet, 1: 372-373, 1976.

T

1078. Taitelman, E., Peer, E., Bursztein, S. and Better, O.S. Coma and
        Plasma Hyperosmolality Due to Ethanol Intoxication. Harefuah,
        93: 144-145, 1977.

1079. Tammaro, A.E. Rilievi reografici in soggetti anziani bevitori in
        confronto a coetanei astemi. [Rheographic Findings in Aged
        Drinkers as Compared with Non-Drinkers of the Same Age.]
        Giornale di Gerontologia, 15: 93-97, 1967.

1080. Tarasiuk, I.K. Vliyaniye zloupotrebleniya alkogolem na razvitiye
        i techeniye ostrykh narushenii mozgovogo krovoobrashcheniya.
        [The Effect of Alcohol Misuse on the Development and Course
        of Acute Brain Circulation Disorders.] Zhurnal Nevropato-
        logii i Psikhiatria Imeni S.S. Korsakova, 76: 1777-1780,
        1976.

1081. Tarter, Ralph E. Psychological Deficit in Chronic Alcoholics: A
        Review. International Journal of the Addictions, 10: 327-368,
        1975.

1082. Tashiro, Michiko and Lipscomb, Wendell R. Mortality Experience of
        Alcoholics. Quarterly Journal of Studies on Alcohol, 24(2):
        203-212, 1963.

1083. Tavel, M.E., Davidson, W. and Batterton, T.D. A Critical Analysis
        of Mortality Associated with Delirium Tremens: Review of
        39 Fatalities in a 9-Year Period. American Journal of Medical
        Science, 242: 18-29, 1961.

1084. Taylor, J.A.T. Metronidazole: A New Agent for Combined Somatic
        and Psychic Therapy of Alcoholism; A Case Study and Prelimin-
        ary Report. Bulletin of the Los Angeles Neurological Society,
        29: 158-162, 1964.

1085. Teeter, Ruth B., Garetz, Floyd K., Miller, Winston R. and Heiland,
        William F. Psychiatric Disturbances of Aged Patients in
        Skilled Nursing Homes. American Journal of Psychiatry,
        133(12): 1430-1434, 1976.

1086. Tepfer, K.S. and Levine, B.A. Covert Sensitization with Internal
       Aversive Cues in the Treatment of Chronic Alcoholism. Psycho-
       logical Reports, 41: 92-94, 1977.

1087. Tessier, J.-F., Lecoublet, D., Serise, M., Bernadou, M., Labadie,
       J.-C. and Freour, P. Le coût social de la tuberculose chez
       les alcooliques et chez les non buveurs; approche théorique--
       essai d'application pratique. [The Social Cost of Tuberculo-
       sis in Alcoholics and Nondrinkers; Theoretical Approach--At-
       tempting a Practical Application.] Revue de l'Alcoolisme, 20:
       89-118, 1974.

1088. Tetu, S. and Shore, D. A Survey of Treatment Needs of Women with
       Drug-Related Problems. Ottawa: Canadian Addictions Foun-
       dation, 1977.

1089. Thabit, W. The Bowery Planning Problem: A Preliminary Report.
       New York, 1972. (Prepared in conjunction with the Bowery
       Planning Task Force under Contract to the Housing and Develop-
       ment Administration, City of New York.)

1090. Thomas, J.V., Ewing, J.A. and Desrosiers, N.A. Alcohol Consump-
       tion and Arcus Senilis: A Search for a Significant Relation-
       ship. British Journal of Addiction, 67: 177-179, 1972.

1091. Thomas-Knight, R. Treating Alcoholism among the Aged: The Ef-
       fectiveness of a Special Treatment Program for Older Problem
       Drinkers. Ph.D. Dissertation, University of Arkansas, 1978.
       (University Microfilms No. 78-23210.)

1092. Thomsen, K. Zinc, Liver Cirrhosis, and Anorexia Nervosa. Acta
       Dermato-Venereologica, 58: 283, 1978.

1093. Thorarinsson, Alma Anna. Mortality among Men Alcoholics in Ice-
       land, 1951-74. Journal of Studies on Alcohol, 40(7): 704-
       718, 1979.

1094. Thorson, James A. and Thorson, Judy R. Patient Education and the
       Older Drug Taker. Journal of Drug Issues, 9(1): 85-89, 1979.

1095. Tideiksaar, R. Postural Hypotension and Diuretic Therapy in the
       Elderly. Canadian Medical Association Journal, 120: 13,
       1979.

1096. Tokuhata, G.K., Digon, E. and Ramaswamy, K. Alcohol Sales and
       Socioeconomic Factors Related to Cirrhosis of the Liver Mor-
       tality in Pennsylvania. HSMHA Health Report, 86: 253-264,
       1971.

1097. Tommasi, M. Degénérescence axiale du corp calleux (syndrome de
       Marchiafava-Bignami) au cours d'une psycho-polynévrite de
       Korsakoff; à propos d'une observation anatomo-clinique.
       [Axial Degeneration of the Corpus Callosum (Marchiafava-
       Bignami Syndrome) in a Case of Korsakoff's Psychosis; Anatomo-
       clinical Observation.] Journal de Médecine de Lyon, 38: 289-
       297, 1957.

1098. Tonge, J.I., O'Reilly, M.J., Davison, A., Johnston, N.G. and Wil-
       key, I.S. Traffic-Crash Fatalities (1968-1973): Injury Pat-
       terns and Other Factors. Medicine, Science, and the Law,
       17(1): 9-24, 1977.

1099. Tongue, Archer. The Past and Present Status of Alcoholism, an
       Overview. In: World Dialogue on Alcohol and Drug Dependence.
       Ed. Elizabeth D. Whitney. Boston: Beacon Press, 1970,
       pages 1-19, especially pages 15-16.

1100. Torry, J.M. A Case of Suicide with Nitrazepam and Alcohol. Prac-
       titioner, 217: 648-649, 1976.

1101. Triggs, E.J., Nation, R.L., Long, A. and Ashley, J.J. Pharmaco-
       kinetics in the Elderly. European Journal of Clinical Phar-
       macology, 8: 55-62, 1975.

1102. Truchet, P., Jacquemond, D. and Benazet, L. Etude statistique de
       l'imprégnation alcoolique des traumatisés admis dans un ser-
       vice de chirurgie. [Statistical Study of Alcoholic Impreg-
       nation of the Injured Admitted to a Surgical Service.] Lyon
       Médical, 215: 903-917, 1966.

1103. Tschersich, A. Klinik, Verlauf und Prognose des alkoholischen
       Korsakow-Syndroms; dargestellt an Hand von 55 eigenen Beo-
       bachtungen. [Clinical Course and Prognosis of Korsakoff's
       Syndrome in Alcoholics; 55 Observations.] Fortschritte der
       Neurologie, Psychiatrie und ihrer Grenzgebiete, 46: 519-563,
       1978.

1104. Turner, Thomas B. Beer and Wine for Geriatric Patients. Journal
       of the American Medical Association, 226(7): 779-780, 1973.

1105. Turpeinen, O. Alkoholmortalitet under Finlands autonoma tid.
       [Alcohol-Related Mortality in Finland during the Era of
       Autonomy.] Alkoholpolitik, 41: 180-183, 1978. (Also as:
       Viinakuolema autonomian ajan Suomessa. [Alcohol Mortality
       during Autonomy in Finland.] Alkoholipolitiikka, 43: 107-
       110, 1978.

1106. Tuyns, A.J. Cancer of the Oesophagus; Further Evidence of the
       Relation to Drinking Habits in France. International Jour-
       nal of Cancer, 5: 152-156, 1970.

1107. Tuyns, A.J., Péquignot, G. and Jensen, O.M. Esophageal Cancer in
       Ille-et-Vilaine in Relation to Levels of Alcohol and Tobacco
       Consumption: Risks Are Multiplying. Bulletin of Cancer,
       64(1): 45-60, 1977.

1108. Twigg, William C. Alcoholism in a Home for the Aged: Commentary
       on a Case History. Geriatrics, 14(6): 391-395, 1959.

1109. Tyndel, M. and Rutherdale, J.A. The Hospital Addiction (Munchau-
       sen) Syndrome and Alcoholism. International Journal of Ad-
       diction, 8: 121-126, 1973.

U

1110. United States. Department of Health, Education, and Welfare.
       Epidemiology of Aging. Ed. Adrian M. Ostfeld, Don C. Gib-
       son, and Christine P. Donnelly. DHEW Publication No. (NIH)
       77-711. Washington, D.C.: U.S. Government Printing Office,
       1972.

1111. United States. Department of Health, Education, and Welfare.
       National Institute on Alcohol Abuse and Alcoholism.
       First Special Report to the U.S. Congress on Alcohol and
       Health from the Secretary of Health, Education, and Welfare.
       Ed. Mark Keller and Shirley Sirota Rosenberg. DHEW Publi-
       cation No. ADM 74-68. Washington, D.C.: U.S. Government
       Printing Office, 1971, pages 23 and 26.

1112. United States. Department of Health, Education, and Welfare.
       National Institute on Alcohol Abuse and Alcoholism.
       Second Special Report to the U.S. Congress on Alcohol and
       Health from the Secretary of Health, Education, and Welfare.
       Ed. Mark Keller. DHEW Publication No. ADM 75-212. Washing-
       ton, D.C.: U.S. Government Printing Office, 1974, pages 27-
       35.

1113. United States. Department of Health, Education, and Welfare.
       National Institute on Alcohol Abuse and Alcoholism.
       Third Special Report to the U.S. Congress on Alcohol and
       Health from the Secretary of Health, Education, and Welfare.
       Ed. Ernest P. Noble. DHEW Publication No. ADM 79-832.
       Washington, D.C.: U.S. Government Printing Office, 1978,
       pages 53-55, 63-67.

1114. United States Senate, Ninety-fourth Congress. Alcohol and Drug
       Abuse among the Elderly. Joint Hearings before the Subcom-
       mittee on Aging and Subcommittee on Alcoholism and Narcotics
       of the Committee on Labor and Public Welfare. Second Session
       on Examination of the Problems of Alcohol and Drug Abuse
       among the Elderly. Washington, D.C.: U.S. Government
       Printing Office, 1976.

1115. Urcaray, L. Polineuritis alcoholica y vitaminoterapia. [Alco-
         holic Polyneuritis and Vitamin Therapy.] Prensa Medica
         Argentina, 28: 2231-2233, 1941.

1116. Uses of Wine in Medical Practice, A Summary. San Francisco, Cali-
         fornia: Wine Advisory Board, 1956.

V

1117. Van der Kolk, Bessel A. Organic Problems in the Aged: Brain Syndromes and Alcoholism. [Introduction.] Journal of Geriatric Psychiatry, 11(2): 131-134, 1978.

1118. Van der Kolk, Bessel A. Organic Problems in the Aged: Brain Syndromes and Alcoholism. [Discussion.] Journal of Geriatric Psychiatry, 11(2): 167-170, 1978.

1119. Van der Kolk, Bessel A. Organic Problems in the Aged: Brain Syndromes and Alcoholism. [Introductory Remarks on Alcoholism.] Journal of Geriatric Psychiatry, 11(2): 171-173, 1978.

1120. Van de Vyvere, Barbara, Hughes, Mary and Fish, David G. The Elderly Chronic Alcoholic: A Practical Approach. Canadian Welfare, 52(4): 9-13, 1976.

1121. Verdy, Maurice and Brouillet, Joffre. Alcohol and Adrenocortical Function: Negative Effect on ACTH Reserve in Man by Metyrapone Test. Quarterly Journal of Studies on Alcohol, 31(3): 545-549, 1970.

1122. Vestal, Robert E., McGuire, Elizabeth A., Tobin, Jordan D., Andres, Reubin, Norris, Arthur H. and Mezey, Esteban. Aging and Ethanol Metabolism. Clinical Pharmacology and Therapeutics, 21(3): 343-354, 1977.

1123. Vestal, Robert E., Norris, Arthur H., Tobin, Jordan D., Cohen, Bernice H., Shock, Nathan W. and Andres, Reubin. Antipyrine Metabolism in Man: Influence of Age, Alcohol, Caffeine, and Smoking. Clinical Pharmacology and Therapeutics, 18(4): 425-432, 1975.

1124. Vickers, Raymond. The Therapeutic Milieu and the Older Depressed Patient. Journal of Gerontology, 31(3): 314-317, 1976.

1125. Victor, Maurice, Adams, Raymond D. and Collins, George H. The
       Wernicke-Korsakoff Syndrome: A Clinical and Pathological
       Study of 245 Patients, 82 with Post-Mortem Examinations.
       Philadelphia, Pennsylvania: F.A. Davis Company, 1971, es-
       pecially pages 2-3, 17-19.

1126. Vidojković, Predrag, Grbeša, Branislav, Miljković, Srbobran and
       Srecković, Miodrag. Alkoholizam starih osoba. [Alcoholism
       in the Aged.] Alkoholizam, 10(3-4): 52-59, 1970.

1127. Viel, B., Salcedo, D., Donoso, S. and Varela, A. Alcoholism,
       Accidents, Atherosclerosis and Hepatic Damage. In: Alcohol
       and Alcoholism. Ed. R.E. Popham. Toronto: Addiction Re-
       search Foundation, 1970, pages 319-337.

1128. Vincent, M.O. Physicians after 65. Canadian Medical Association
       Journal, 120: 998, 1001, 1979.

1129. Vincent, R.G. and Marchetta, F. The Relationship of the Use of
       Tobacco and Alcohol to Cancer of the Oral Cavity, Pharynx,
       or Larynx. American Journal of Surgery, 106: 501-505, 1963.

1130. Vogel-Sprott, M. Defining "Light" and "Heavy" Social Drinking:
       Research Implications and Hypotheses. Quarterly Journal of
       Studies on Alcohol, 35(4): 1388-1392, 1974.

1131. Vojtěchovský, M., Brezinová, V., Šimáně, Z. and Hort, V. An Ex-
       perimental Approach to Sleep and Aging. Human Development,
       12: 64-72, 1969.

1132. Volpe, Anne and Kastenbaum, Robert. Beer and TLC. American Jour-
       nal of Nursing, 67: 100-103, 1967.

1133. Vuga, D. L'alcool nella tuberculosi polmonare dell'anziano. [Al-
       cohol in Pulmonary Tuberculosis of the Aged.] Policlinico
       Sezione Pratica, 73: 264-267, 1966.

W

1134. Wadstein, J. and Skude, G. Does Hypokalaemia Precede Delirium Tremens? The Lancet, 2(8089): 549-550, 1978.

1135. Waern, U. Health and Disease at the Age of Sixty: Findings in a Health Survey of 60-Year-Old Men in Uppsala and a Comparison with Men Ten Years Younger. Uppsala Journal of Medical Sciences, 83: 153-162, 1978.

1136. Waern, U., Boberg, J. and Hellsing, K. Evaluation of Indices of Alcohol Intake in a Population of 60-Year-Old Men in Uppsala, Sweden. Acta Medica Scandinavica, 205: 353-360, 1979.

1137. Waldron, Ingrid. Why Do Women Live Longer than Men? Social Science and Medicine, 10: 349-362, 1976.

1138. Wallace, Jean G. Drinkers and Abstainers in Norway: A National Survey. Quarterly Journal of Studies on Alcohol (Supplement No. 6): 129-151, 1972.

1139. Waller, Julian A. Factors Associated with Alcohol and Responsibility for Fatal Highway Crashes. Quarterly Journal of Studies on Alcohol, 33(1): 160-170, 1972.

1140. Waller, Julian A. Identification of Problem Drinking among Drunken Drivers. Journal of the American Medical Association, 200: 114-120, 1967.

1141. Waller, Julian A. Injury in Aged: Clinical and Epidemiological Implications. New York State Journal of Medicine, 74(12): 2200-2208, 1974.

1142. Waller, Julian A., King, E.M., Nielson, G. and Turkel, H.W. Alcohol and Other Factors in California Highway Fatalities. Journal of Forensic Science, 14: 429-444, 1969.

1143. Waller, Julian A. and Turkel, H.W. Alcoholism and Traffic Deaths. New England Journal of Medicine, 275: 532-536, 1966.

1144. Wallerstedt, S. On the Applicability of Statements on Drinking
       and Dietary Habits for the Calculation of Risks or Organ Dam-
       age in Chronic Alcoholics. Acta Hepato-Gastroenterologica,
       25: 275-278, 1978.

1145. Wallgren, H. and Forsander, O. Effect of Adaptation to Alcohol
       and of Age on Voluntary Consumption of Alcohol by Rats.
       British Journal of Nutrition, 17(4): 453-457, 1963.

1146. Wallis, W.E., Willoughby, E. and Baker, P. Coma in the Wernicke-
       Korsakoff Syndrome. The Lancet, 2: 400-401, 1978.

1147. Walsh, A.C. and Lukas, E. Alcoholic Brain Damage: Anticoagulant
       Therapy. Journal of the American Geriatrics Society, 22:
       555-556, 1974.

1148. Walter, G.F. Marchiafava-Bignami Disease; First Case in Germany.
       Archiv für Psychiatrie und Nervenkrankheiten, 226: 75-78,
       1978.

1149. Wanamaker, William M. and Skillman, Thomas G. Motor Nerve Con-
       duction in Alcoholics. Quarterly Journal of Studies on Alco-
       hol, 27(1): 16-22, 1966.

1150. Warder, J. and Ross, C.J. Age and Alcoholism. British Journal
       of Addiction, 66(1): 45-51, 1971.

1151. Warkov, Seymour, Bacon, Selden D. and Hawkins, Arthur C. Social
       Correlates of Industrial Problem Drinking. Quarterly Journal
       of Studies on Alcohol, 26(1): 58-71, 1965.

1152. Warren, R. and Simpson, H.M. Impaired Driving. (Technical Re-
       port Series No. 8; article also in French.) Ottawa: Depart-
       ment of National Health and Welfare, 1978.

1153. Watkin, Donald M. Role of Alcoholic Beverages in Gerontology.
       In: Fermented Food Beverages in Nutrition. Nutrition Foun-
       dation: A Monograph Series. International Symposium on Fer-
       mented Food Beverages in Nutrition, Mayo Clinic, Rochester,
       Minnesota, June 15-17, 1977. Ed. C.F. Gastineau, W.J. Darby,
       and T.B. Turner. New York: Academic Press, 1979, pages 225-
       243.

1154. Wautier, J.-L. La thrombopénie au cours des intoxications al-
       cooliques; son mécanisme. [Thrombopenia during Alcohol
       Intoxication; Its Mechanism.] Revue de l'Alcoolisme, 20:
       169-184, 1974.

1155. Weaver, G.A. and Kleinman, M.S. Gastric Polyposis Due to Multiple
       Hyperplastic Adenomatous Polyps. American Journal of Diges-
       tive Diseases, 23(4): 346-352, 1978.

1156. Webb, J.D. The Older Hospitalized Alcoholic: An Assessment of
       His Mood and Food Consumption Patterns. Ph.D. Dissertation,
       Cornell University, 1978. (University Microfilms No. 78-
       17815.)

1157. Webb, R.A.J., Egger, G.J. and Reynolds, I. Prediction and Preven-
          tion of Drug Abuse. Journal of Drug Education, 8: 221-230,
          1978.

1158. Wechsler, David. The Effect of Alcohol on Mental Activity. Quar-
          terly Journal of Studies on Alcohol, 2(3): 479-485, 1941.

1159. Wechsler, Henry, Demone, Harold W., Jr. and Gottlieb, N. Drinking
          Patterns of Greater Boston Adults: Subgroups Differences on
          the QFV Index. Journal of Studies on Alcohol, 39(7): 1158-
          1165, 1978.

1160. Wechsler, Henry, Thum, Denise, Demone, Harold W., Jr. and Dwin-
          nell, Joanne. Social Characteristics and Blood Alcohol
          Level: Measurements of Subgroup Differences. Quarterly
          Journal of Studies on Alcohol, 33(1): 132-147, 1972.

1161. Weiner, Sheldon and Weaver, Lelon. Begging and Social Deviance
          on Skid Row. Quarterly Journal of Studies on Alcohol, 35(4):
          1307-1315, 1974.

1162. Weinlander, Max M. Alcoholics and the Influence of Age on the
          Variables of the Structured-Objective Rorschach Test (SORT).
          Journal of Psychology, 65: 57-58, 1967.

1163. Weissman, M.M., Sholomskas, D., Pottenger, M., Prusoff, B.A. and
          Locke, Ben Z. Assessing Depressive Symptoms in Five Psychi-
          atric Populations: A Validation Study. American Journal of
          Epidemiology, 106(3): 203-214, 1977.

1164. Wellman, Wayne M., Maxwell, Milton A. and O'Hollaren, Paul. Pri-
          vate Hospital Alcoholic Patients and the Changing Conception
          of the "Typical" Alcoholic. Quarterly Journal of Studies on
          Alcohol, 18(3): 388-404, 1955.

1165. Werner, W. Schlafstörungen des alternden und alten Menschen.
          [Sleep Disorders in the Aging and Aged.] Zeitschrift für
          Allgemeinmedizin, 53(33): 2078-2084, 1977.

1166. Westie, Katharine S. and McBride, Duane, C. The Effects of Eth-
          nicity, Age and Sex upon Processing through an Emergency
          Alcohol Health Care Delivery System. British Journal of
          Addiction, 74: 21-29, 1979.

1167. Whisky for Persons with "Strokes." (Queries and Minor Notes.)
          Journal of the American Medical Association, 146: 1274,
          1951.

1168. Whitehead, P.C. and Szandorowska, B. Introduction of Low Alcohol
          Content Beer: A Test of the Addiction-Substitution Hypothe-
          sis. Journal of Studies on Alcohol, 38(11): 2157-2164, 1977.

1169. Whitfield, C.L., Thompson, G., Lamb, A., Spencer, V., Pfeifer, M.
       and Browning-Ferrando, M. Detoxification of 1,024 Alcoholic
       Patients without Psychoactive Drugs. Journal of the Amer-
       ican Medical Association, 239(14): 1409-1410, 1978.

1170. Whittier, John R. and Korenyi, Charles. Selected Characteristics
       of Aged Patients: A Study of Mental Hospital Admissions.
       Comprehensive Psychiatry, 2(2): 113-120, 1961.

1171. Whitty, C.W.M. Loss of Memory as a Clinical Problem. British
       Journal of Hospital Medicine, 20: 276, 279-280, 283-284,
       1978.

1172. Wiberg, G. Stuart, Samson, J.M., Maxwell, W.B., Coldwell, Blake B.
       and Trenholm, H. Locksley. Further Studies on the Acute
       Toxicity of Ethanol in Young and Old Rats: Relative Impor-
       tance of Pulmonary Excretion and Total Body Water. Toxi-
       cology and Applied Pharmacology, 20: 22-29, 1971.

1173. Wiberg, G. Stuart, Trenholm, H. Locksley and Coldwell, Blake B.
       Increased Ethanol Toxicity in Old Rats: Changes in LD50,
       in Vivo and in Vitro Metabolism, and Liver Alcohol Dehydro-
       genase Activity. Toxicology and Applied Pharmacology, 16:
       718-727, 1970.

1174. Wiederholt, W.C., Kobayashi, R.M., Stockard, J.J. and Rossiter,
       V.S. Central Pontine Myelinolysis; a Clinical Reappraisal.
       Archives of Neurology, 34: 220-223, 1977.

1175. Wieth, J.O. and Jorgenssen, H.E. Treatment of Methanol and Eth-
       anol Poisoning with Hemodialysis. Danish Medical Bulletin,
       8: 103-106, 1961.

1176. Wiik-Larsen, E. and Enger, E. Medikament- og alkoholdødsfall i
       og utenfor sykehus i Oslo på grunn av akutt selvpåført fir-
       giftning. [Death by Acute Self-Poisoning with Drugs and Al-
       cohol In and Outside Hospital in Oslo.] Tidsskrift for den
       Norske Laegeforening, 98: 371-373, 1978.

1177. Wiik-Larsen, E., Saltvedt, E., Skuterud, B. and Enger, E. Socio-
       logical and Psychiatric Aspects of 232 Poisonings. Tids-
       skrift for den Norske Laegeforening, 97(5): 232-234, 1977.

1178. Wiklund, Rt. Hon. Daniel, M.P. Proposal Prepared by a Government
       Commission in Sweden. In: Proceedings of an International
       Symposium on The Drunkenness Offence held from 15 to 17 May,
       1968, at the Institute of Psychiatry, Maudsley Hospital,
       London, S.E.5. under the Auspices of Camberwell Council on
       Alcoholism and International Council on Alcohol and Addic-
       tions. Ed. Timothy Cook, Dennis Gath, and Celia Hensman.
       Oxford: Pergamon Press, 1969, pages 127-134, especially
       pages 128-129.

1179. Wilkins, R.H. The Hidden Alcoholic in Medical Practice. London:
       Elek Science, 1974.

1180. Wilkinson, D. Adrian and Carlen, Peter L. Neuropsychological
       and Neurological Assessment of Alcoholism: Discrimination
       between Groups of Alcoholics. Journal of Studies on Alcohol,
       41(1): 129-139, 1980.

1181. Wilkinson, Patricia. Alcoholism in the Aged. Journal of Ger-
       iatrics, 2(4): 59-64, 1971.

1182. Williams, Erma Polly and Mysak, Patricia. Community Agency
       Study. Alcoholism and Problem Drinking among Older Persons.
       New Brunswick, New Jersey: Center of Alcohol Studies, Rut-
       gers University, 1973.

1183. Williams, Jack D., Ray, Charles G. and Overall, John E. Mental
       Aging and Organicity in an Alcoholic Population. Journal of
       Consulting and Clinical Psychology, 41(3): 392-396, 1973.

1184. Williams, M. and Owen G. Word vs. Picture Recognition in Amnesic
       and Aphasic Patients. Neuropsychologia, 15: 351-354, 1977.

1185. Williams, Phyllis H. and Straus, Robert. Drinking Patterns of
       Italians in New Haven: Utilization of the Personal Diary as
       a Research Technique. II. Diaries 3, 4 and 5. Quarterly
       Journal of Studies on Alcohol, 11(2): 250-308, 1950.

1186. Williams, Phyllis H. and Straus, Robert. Drinking Patterns of
       Italians in New Haven: Utilization of the Personal Diary as
       a Research Technique. IV. Diaries 8, 9 and 10; Summary and
       Conclusions. Quarterly Journal of Studies on Alcohol, 11(4):
       586-629, 1950.

1187. Williams, R.R. and Horm, J.W. Association of Cancer Sites with
       Tobacco and Alcohol Consumption and Socioeconomic Status of
       Patients: Interview Study from the Third National Cancer
       Survey. Journal of the National Cancer Institute, 58(3):
       525-547, 1977.

1188. Williams, R.R., Stegens, N.L., and Goldsmith, J.R. Associations
       of Cancer Site and Type with Occupation and Industry from
       the Third National Cancer Survey Interview. Journal of the
       National Cancer Institute, 59(4): 1147-1185, 1977.

1189. Williams, Roger J. Biochemical Individuality Affects Patterns
       of Aging. In: The Crisis in Health Care for the Aging.
       Ed. Leon Summit. New York: National Conference of the Hux-
       ley Institute for Biosocial Research, 1972, pages 42-43.

1190. Wilson, Arthur S., Barboriak, Joseph J.F. and Kass, Warren A.
       Effects of Alcoholic Beverages and Conceners on Psychomotor
       Skills in Old and Young Subjects. Quarterly Journal of
       Studies on Alcohol (Supplement No. 5): 115-129, 1970.

1191. Wilson, Arthur S., Mabry, Edward A., Khavari, Khalil A. and Dalpes,
       Dennis. Discriminant Analysis of MMPI Profiles for Demo-
       graphic Classifications of Male Alcoholics. Journal of
       Studies on Alcohol, 38(1): 47-57, 1977.

1192. Wilson, J. and Manton, K. Localism and Temperance. _Sociology_
       and Social Research, 59: 121-135, 1975.

1193. Wingerd, J. and Sponzilli, E.E. Concentrations of Serum Protein
       Fractions in White Women: Effects of Age, Weight, Smoking,
       Tonsillectomy, and Other Factors. _Clinical Chemistry_, 23:
       1310-1317, 1977.

1194. Wolff, G. Does Alcohol Cause Chronic Gastritis? _Scandinavian_
       Journal of Gastroenterology, 5: 289-291, 1970.

1195. Wolff, K. _The Emotional Rehabilitation of the Geriatric Patient._
       Springfield, Illinois: C.C. Thomas, 1970.

1196. Wolff, Sulammith and Holland, Lydia. A Questionnaire Follow-up of
       Alcoholic Patients. _Quarterly Journal of Studies on Alcohol_,
       25: 108-118, 1964.

1197. Wood, H.P. and Flippin, H.F. "Delirium Tremens" Following With-
       drawal of Ethclorvinol. _American Journal of Psychiatry_, 121:
       1127-1129, 1965.

1198. Wood, W. Gibson. The Elderly Alcoholic: Some Diagnostic Problems
       and Considerations. In: _The Clinical Psychology of Aging_.
       Ed. M. Storandt, I.C. Siegler, and M.F. Elias. New York and
       London: Plenum Press, 1978.

1199. Wozniak, Kenneth J. and Silverman, Eugene M. Granulocytic Adher-
       ence in Chronic Alcoholism. _American Journal of Clinical_
       Pathology, 71(3): 269-272, 1979.

1200. Wynne, Ronald D. and Heller, Frank. Drug Overuse among the Elder-
       ly: A Growing Problem. _Perspectives on Aging_, 11(2): 15-18,
       1973.

Y

1201. Yaksich, S., Jr. AAA Launches Alcohol-Traffic Program for Senior Citizens. Traffic Safety, 78(8): 21, 1978.

1202. Yamamuro, Bufo. Alcoholism in Tokyo. Quarterly Journal of Studies on Alcohol, 34(3): 950-954, 1973.

1203. Yamane, Hideo, Katoh, Nobukatsu and Fujita, Tamotsu. Characteristics of Three Groups of Men Alcoholics Differentiated by Age at First Admission for Alcoholism Treatment in Japan. Journal of Studies on Alcohol, 41(1): 100-103, 1980.

1204. Yano, Katsuhiko, Rhoads, George G. and Kagan, Abraham. Coffee, Alcohol and Risk of Coronary Heart Disease among Japanese Men Living in Hawaii. The New England Journal of Medicine, 297(8): 405-409, 1977.

1205. Yano, Katsuhiko, Rhoads, George G. and Kagan, Abraham. Epidemiology of Serum Uric Acid among Japanese-American Men in Hawaii. Journal of Chronic Disease, 30(3): 171-184, 1977.

Z

1206. Zax, Melvin, Gardner, Elmer A. and Hart, William T. A Survey of the Prevalence of Alcoholism in Monroe County, N.Y., 1961. Quarterly Journal of Studies on Alcohol, 28(2): 316-327, 1967.

1207. Zax, Melvin, Gardner, Elmer A. and Hart, William T. Public Intoxication in Rochester: A Survey of Individuals Charged during 1961. Quarterly Journal of Studies on Alcohol, 25(4): 669-678, 1964.

1208. Zax, Melvin, Marsey, Ruth and Biggs, Charles F. Demographic Characteristics of Alcoholic Outpatients and the Tendency to Remain in Treatment. Quarterly Journal of Studies on Alcohol, 22(1): 98-105, 1961.

1209. Zeichner, A.M. Alcoholism as a Defense against Social Isolation. Case Reports of Clinical Psychology, 2(2): 51-59, 1951.

1210. Zemek, P. and Drdková, S. Sebevražedné jednání v opilosti. [Suicidal Behavior in Drunkenness.] Sbornik Lekarsky, 80: 153-159, 1978.

1211. Zenkevich, G.S. and Maistro, P. Ya. Nekotoryye morfologicheskiye osobennosti alkogol'noi entsefalopatii Gaiye-Vernike i voprosy yeye sektsionnoi diagnostiki. [Some Morphological Characteristics of Gayeț-Wernicke's Alcoholic Encephalopathy and Some of the Problems of Its Postmortem Diagnosis.] Zhurnal Nevropatologii i Psikhiatrii Imeni S.S. Korsakova, 75: 1036-1040, 1975.

1212. Zimberg, Sheldon. Alcohol and the Elderly. In: Drugs and the Elderly: Social and Pharmacological Issues. Ed. D.M. Petersen, F.J. Whittington, and B.P. Payne. Springfield, Illinois: Charles C. Thomas, 1979, pages 28-40.

1213. Zimberg, Sheldon. Diagnosis and Treatment of the Elderly Alcoholic. Alcoholism, 2(1): 27-29, 1978.

1214. Zimberg, Sheldon. Evaluation of Alcoholism Treatment in Harlem.
       Quarterly Journal of Studies on Alcohol, 35(2): 550-557,
       1974.

1215. Zimberg, Sheldon. Outpatient Geriatric Psychiatry in an Urban
       Ghetto with Nonprofessional Workers. American Journal of
       Psychiatry, 125: 1697-1702, 1969.

1216. Zimberg, Sheldon. Principles of Alcoholism Psychotherapy. In:
       Practical Approaches to Alcoholism Psychotherapy. Ed. Shel-
       don Zimberg, John Wallace, and Sheila Blume. New York:
       Plenum Press, 1978, pages 3-18.

1217. Zimberg, Sheldon. Psychiatric Office Treatment of Alcoholism. In:
       Practical Approaches to Alcoholism Psychotherapy. Ed. Shel-
       don Zimberg, John Wallace, and Sheila Blume. New York:
       Plenum Press, 1978, pages 47-62.

1218. Zimberg, Sheldon. Psychosocial Treatment of Elderly Alcohol-
       ics. In: Practical Approaches to Alcoholism Psychother-
       apy. Ed. Sheldon Zimberg, John Wallace, and Sheila Blume.
       New York: Plenum Press, 1978, pages 237-251.

1219. Zimberg, Sheldon. The Elderly Alcoholic. Gerontologist, 13(3):
       57, 1973.

1220. Zimberg, Sheldon. The Elderly Alcoholic. Gerontologist, 14(3):
       221-224, 1974.

1221. Zimberg, Sheldon. The Geriatric Alcoholic on a Psychiatric Couch.
       Geriatric Focus, 11(5): 1, 6-7, 1972.

1222. Zimberg, Sheldon. The Psychiatrist and Medical Home Care: Geri-
       atric Psychiatry in the Harlem Community. American Journal
       of Psychiatry, 127: 1062-1066, 1971.

1223. Zimberg, Sheldon. Treatment of Socioeconomically Deprived Alco-
       holics. In: Practical Approaches to Alcoholism Psychother-
       apy. Ed. Sheldon Zimberg, John Wallace, and Sheila Blume.
       New York: Plenum Press, 1978, pages 205-218.

1224. Zimberg, Sheldon. Treatment of the Elderly Alcoholic in the Com-
       munity and in an Institutional Setting. Addictive Diseases,
       3(3): 417-427, 1978.

1225. Zimberg, Sheldon. Two Types of Problem Drinkers: Both Can Be
       Managed. Geriatrics, 29(8): 135-138, 1974.

1226. Zung, B.J. Sociodemographic Correlates of Problem Drinking among
       DWI Offenders. Journal of Studies on Alcohol, 40: 1064-1072,
       1979.

1227. Zylman, Richard. Accidents, Alcohol and Single-Cause Explan-
       ations: Lessons from the Grand Rapids Study. Quarterly
       Journal of Studies on Alcohol (Supplement 4): 212-233,
       1968.

1228. Zylman, Richard. Age Is More Important than Alcohol in the Col-
       lision-Involvement of Young and Old Drivers. Journal of
       Traffic Safety Education, 20(1): 7-8, 34, 1972.

Subject Index

The numbers in this index refer to entry numbers, not page numbers.

About the Compilers

GRACE M. BARNES, ERNEST L. ABEL, and CHARLES A. S. ERNST are affiliated with the New York State Research Institute on Alcoholism, Buffalo, New York.